The Selected Writings of Mark Pettinelli
(The Difference between Feelings and
Thoughts)

The Selected Writings of Mark Pettinelli (The Difference between Feelings and Thoughts)

Mark Rozen Pettinelli

CONTENTS

1 1 1

The Selected Writings of Mark Pettinelli
By
Mark Pettinelli

2021

Some Notes about Logic
By
Mark Pettinelli

So there is an emotion concept and a thought concept. Instead I mean there is an emotion process and a thought process. The thought process involves people thinking, and the emotion process involves people feeling.

There are also concepts that the person can think about, those concepts are part of the thought process. For instance someone could be having a stream of thought that involves thinking about different concepts. What kind of concepts could someone be thinking about?

Well I mean, a stream of thought could involve various different concepts that the person could be thinking about. There is also an emotion process, which involves a person having a steady stream of feelings, which could occur at the same time as a thought process.

What could make the thought process complicated? It could contain complicated thoughts, or complicated feelings as part of the feeling process.

Um so I'm trying to figure out what to write. This could be a sort of final article of sorts. I mean I've done most of my research already, the only thing left is to figure out what to write next. I can think clearly, I follow my emotional processes and my thought processes, and there are concepts that I am aware of. I mean the mind thinks with concepts and thoughts and it feels emotions all of the time.

If the mind feels emotions and thinks about or with thoughts all of the time, then what else would I need to know? Thinking isn't that complicated, neither is feeling things. I mean I feel things all the time and it isn't complicated.

It really isn't complicated, like I mean a thought is just a thought, and a feeling is just a feeling. That's fairly simple. There's also concepts in the mind, or concepts that you think about. Some of the concepts could be complicated but they're still just concepts. Most concepts are simple I would say, however some concepts could be complex.

So what else should I write about, I want to learn more stuff. I don't know what else I could learn though, I mean I know that the mind thinks with concepts and that there is a thought process and an emotion process.

The thought process consists of the person just thinking about stuff, while the emotion process involves the person feeling things, or their steady stream of feelings. There's also concepts that the person can think about.

What would be an example of a concept that the person is thinking about. Going to war with another country is a concept. A democratic or communist government is also a concept. There are lots of different concepts someone can think about, I mean, practically everything someone thinks could be considered to be a concept.

So how would I break down a stream of thought then, or a stream of cognitive processes including both thoughts and feelings. CBT, or cognitive behavioral therapy, involves tracking how one's feelings lead to thoughts, and thoughts lead to behaviors, or any of those occurring in any order.

So it's a fairly simple process, humans have thought processes and emotional processes, or processes involving feelings. That seems fairly simple, I mean the thoughts could involve feeling things, or could involve reasoning about concepts or ideas. WHile the emotions could just involve feeling different things.

Um, so that seems pretty simple, there's either feelings or thoughts, one or the other that someone could be feeling. They could also think while they are feeling things, but that is rather obvious. I mean obviously people can think about things and feel things at the same time.

Is there anything else I need to say about emotions and thoughts? I mean either it's a thought or it's a feeling. When someone is feeling something, what does that feel like? ANd when someone is thinking about something, what does that feel like?

Is there some sort of reasoning process involved with thinking where the person uses logic to check the truthfulness or validity or accuracy of their thoughts? Or is thinking more simple?

Um, so what else am I supposed to write, I've already explained how simple the thought process is, and the feeling process. Those are both mental processes, the other mental processes are perception, memory, language, and attention.

The perception mental process is also simple, thats just the person seeing things and understanding the visuals. The memory process is also simple, that's just things pulled up from memory. The attention process is more complicated and involves the thought process and the feeling process, obviously because you can increase or decrease your attention depending on your emotions or thoughts.

That is, your emotions can influence your attention on something, and so can your thoughts. That's kind of important to know. I mean people pay attention to things, then they can think about or feel what they are paying attention to. That's three of the mental processes right there, feeling, attention and the thought processes.

For instance, if you are being emotional that is going to change what you are paying attention to, or how much attention you are paying to something. A person's thought process might also interfere with their attention. I mean when someone pays attention to something they can focus on it more, direct their thoughts toward it, or direct their vision towards it.

That seems pretty basic, I mean obviously people either think things or feel things. It's also interesting, for instance, is it any more complicated than feeling something and thinking something at the same time? Sometimes I suppose feelings could come along with thoughts at the same time, while other times a thought could create or lead to a feeling, or a feeling could lead to a thought.

Thoughts could also be more complicated, while I would say that feelings are simple, thoughts could be more complex because you could have a complicated concept that you are thinking about or a stream of thought could be complicated say if you were reading something there could be many ideas that you are trying to put together.

ALso with thoughts there is problem solving and decision making, problem solving often leads to the person reaching a conclusion or making a decision. Thats part of some thought processes. What other thought processes are there other than problem solving and decision making?

It would seem that mostly people try to make decision or figure out stuff or problem solve, I mean, what else could someone be doing or thinking about? That's an interesting question.

It's intellectual, I learned a lot of stuff. There's books in my room about cognitive psychology and cognitive science, not that there's that big a difference between them. I thought cognitive science was more about how the mind is structured and how it works with it's neurology, while cognitive psychology was just about the minds mental processes, however if cognitive psychology is about the minds mental processes, then it is also about how the mind works and how it's structured.

I also realized what a concept is, a concept is an idea or thought in your head, it could be about anything but is a coherent idea or thought. It could be a representation of an object in the world, or any general idea really. That makes me think, what kind of ideas does the mind think with - theres ideas about people, ideas about objects, and ideas about anything. Ideas can be emotional or intellectual if you think about it.

An intellectual idea could be a concept about a subject like math or politics. Ideas can be about physical things like how your body feels, or they could be ideas about how you are thinking or the state that your mind is in. Mind and body are connected, however, so I would think it's safe to say that if your mind is feeling some way, then your body is going to respond.

So what else do I know, I mean, i've learned about what a concept is, what an idea is, what a thought is, and what a feeling is. What else would I have to explore? I mean I think I'm fairly logical and clear thinking. It's hard to be clear thinking sometimes if you're being emotional and stuff. If someone is being emotional, then it might be harder for them to think. I said, however, that I am perfectly logical and clear thinking. All the thoughts I have are logical ones, and I understand what is going on. I seem to be on top of things and know what I am doing in addition to being logical and clear thinking.

So what else do I need to explore, that is the question. I started with my psychology of emotions and thoughts book in 2007, now it's 2021 so that means its been about 13 years since I started doing research.

I mean, what led to my being clear thinking now. Was it my understanding of how concepts work in the mind? I have a good understanding of cognitive psychology and cognitive science. I understand emotions and thoughts, and how I experience them. That's pretty much all I need in order to function with feelings. If I have feelings, then I should be able to function and think clearly, I mean I understand that those are feelings, and that I can still think with thoughts.

Thoughts can be complicated if the thought is about a complicated concept or idea, however. But I'm perfectly clearly thinking now, I've always been a clear thinker but before I didn't have this many emotions, or this intense of emotion. So what else do I have to say? I mean I know how to think clearly, I have a steady stream of concepts that goes through my head that I think about constantly. There's ideas, thoughts and concepts that run through my consciousness all the time.

What could interrupt my consciousness or my stream of thought then? I also do stuff like watch tv or listen to music. Consciousness is pretty interesting if you think about it.

I mean, I want to become more intelligent, but I don't know what to explore next. I've already explored cognitive psychology, emotions, thoughts, consciousness, concepts and ideas, and logic. WHat else would I need to research or understand, that is the question.

Um, so I'm trying to figure out what i should research or think about next. I already know cognitive science and how the mind works, I also know logic and concepts, and how those work in the mind. I think perfectly fine and logically. I have a steady stream of thoughts all the time that's perfectly clear, and makes perfectly good sense. I'm intelligent and know what I am doing. There was a bunch of times i went to the emergency room and was not clear thinking, but I got over that and now am clear thinking all of the time. I don't know what else I would need to research here lol. I think I'm doing a fine job with running my life, I don't know if there's any more information I need in order to function or even develop myself more.

I mean, if I can think clearly, then what else would I need to know? That's kind of an important question. I've already done a lot of research that has taught me about cognitive psychology, logic, concepts, cognition and emotion, and other topics. That research and that understanding that I currently have seems perfectly sufficient. I mean I know what logic is - i've looked at a couple of logic textbooks. I also know how the mind works because I've read a bunch of cognitive psychology textbooks.

Theres only a few mental processes like attention, perception, memory, emotion, language, deciding, thinking and reasoning, Those are important mental processes. Part of the mental process of thinking involves logic and concepts. I also understand that I use emotion regulation - which is part of the process of emotion.

As a child I did not understand that I could control or influence my emotions, I didn't even realize that I had many emotions to begin with. Now I am more self-aware and know when I'm having an emotion and what I can do about it.

I have a lot of books in my room, what else do I need to learn from these books? I've already pointed out in this article of notes that I am clear thinking and understand cognitive psychology. I have some cognitive psychology textbooks that talk about the mental processes of attention, memory, perception, emotion, language, and deciding, thinking and reasoning. I also have some textbooks on emotion and cognition. The relationship between emotion and cognition is extremely important. That's basically all the mind is doing, either thinking about something or feeling something, or both.

People also make appraisals of their emotional state. The appraisal is cognitive, while it's about your emotions.

So what else do I need to know or understand? I mean, what else am I supposed to learn? I already know how the mind works through my understanding of cognitive psychology and the mental processes. That gives me a good idea as to how I think and what I need to know in order to think clearly. What else do I need to know? Logic is important, I still have to go through some logic textbooks. But what could they say about logic? I mean logic is fairly simple, I mean i know if what I am thinking makes sense, is logical and valid. I don't really ever think something that is inaccurate, I can keep track of all my thoughts and know if something is inaccurate or if I should think differently about something.

I mean, what is logic exactly, I said before that I was clear thinking and all my thoughts were logical. However, is there more to logic than figuring out if each thought the person thinks makes sense? What other processes are involved. There's problem solving and decision making, for instance. With decision making the person is thinking to arrive at a conclusion, and with problem solving the person is trying to figure out something or trying to come to a solution or a conclusion, which could also be part of decision making.

So thinking doesn't just involve simple thoughts, it involves the mental processes of problem solving and decision making. I mean, what kinds of thoughts do I need to have in order to be logical, or what are all the situations where I would need to think clearly. What would need to be analyzed.

Language would need to be analyzed because people think with language, also every situation they are in, what language they are hearing from outside their mind (like what other people are saying), and any problems they have about what is going on in the world around them or even internal problems they have that they are thinking about (with language).

That pretty much takes care of everything, if i'm on top of my internal thinking, and how my thoughts relate to what is going on around me and if i'm being logical, then I pretty much have everything figured out. So there is thinking, problem solving and decision making. Problem solving might wind up with the person making a decision, and so could other types of thinking.

I mean, how do I know if I am using logic in my thinking. If I have a thought is that thought a sentence in my head? Or is it some type of logical argument? I didn't think before if each thought I had was logical, I simply thought logically without understanding that it made sense. I mean what is the point of thinking if it doesn't make any sense?

So I'm trying to think, if i understand how the mind works, or understand cognitive science and psychology, then what else would I need to know? Clear thinking is a mental process, or I mean just thinking is one of the mental processes. However, there is more to thinking than just thinking clearly, people can problem solve and make decisions also; They can look at information and decide if its important or helpful to them or truthful and valid or if it's false information of little importance.

I mean, if i know what cognitive science is then I know how the mind works. How could I explain here how the mind works then? It appears to me that there is either thought or feeling, and these are the minds two primary functions. People can also perceive visuals or pay attention to things that are either in their head or in the external world.

So I'm trying to explaining how the mind works right. There is more to each of those mental processes I listed. For instance the mental process of thought could involve thinking clear or not thinking clearly. That could be connected to other mental processes such as the person's emotions and their attention or perception or memory. Also, language is important because it is how thought is processed in the mind.

So, like I said, I'm trying to describe how the mind works, or in other words, how the mental processes work like what cognitive psychology and cognitive science are about. I think i've simplified it by just saying that theres emotions and thoughts in the mind. Attention can be influenced by emotions, and it can also be controlled by thoughts.

That seems like a pretty good overview of how the mind functions. Emotions influence thought, attention, and perception while thoughts can also influence those things. That seems like a simplification about how the mind functions, however.

That's how I've been functioning most of my life though. I have a simple train of thought and simple emotions and function perfectly fine. Sometimes I have anxiety or stress and sometimes I'm happy. Emotions and thoughts are simple that way I suppose.

What else would I need to research then? If I am thinking logically then I am functioning perfectly fine and thinking and feeling in an efficient manner. I don't know what else to say about that.

Logic is interesting, is it just thinking clearly? Or what else is involved with logic, how do those processes play out in the mind. Well, for starters, in order to think you have to use a language. Then you have to think out whatever is going on. That seems like it could be fairly simple.

One example I have is at my birthday party when I was about 7 at our beach house in East Haven, CT. I was sitting at the table and they were singing happy to Mark. I was wondering if I should sing along with them and sing 'happy birthday to Mark, happy birthday to you", or if i should sing "happy birthday to me" or just not sing at all. THat was some of the thoughts I was having.

Now I would say to myself, 'well that's a social concept, do they want me to sing along with them or would that be awkward since i'm the birthday boy and i'm supposed to be honored. There are a lot of complicated concepts here, for instance it's a social concept because I have to get in the other people's minds and try to figure out if they want me to sing with them. I was not aware of that when I was 7 years old, I am now aware of that.

Social concepts can be complicated. Another concept I had as a child that I remember when I was also about 7 years old was the when the old lady across the street was babysitting me. She pointed out that the role of paper with the thicker center had more tape because it had a thicker center, I wasn't aware of that but she taught me, I thought the role with the smaller center had more tape. That is also about a concept, but that is a physics concept I learned.

So those are two interesting concepts I had as a child. As a child I didn't understand anything about emotions, now I'm aware that other people have emotions and have some understanding of what is going on in their heads. As a child I did not have that understanding, I just thought with simple concepts and did not understand anything complicated. Now I understand a lot of complicated stuff in different subject areas, like I understand basic algebra and mathematics, I understand what 'emotion regulation' means. Emotion regulation is someone regulating or maintaining their own emotions. As a child I had no clue when I was experiencing an emotion, or if I was experiencing an emotion. Now I understand what an emotion is and if i'm experiencing one.

Concepts are extremely important. Humans think with concepts all the time. Concepts are ideas that the person has in their head. People also think with language. Not all thought is done with words, however. I don't know the exact details but it seems like humans think with a mix of words and understanding that does not need to be expressed with words.

That's kind of complicated, I mean how do I know if the understanding or concept needs to be expressed or thought out with words or not with words? For instance with the racquet game I play when I swing my racquet I don't know how to explain the stroke with words, its a complicated physical movement I don't know how to explain it. That's an example of an understanding that does not use words to explain. WHen i swing the racquet and hit the ball it's physical memory, not verbal concepts.

What about the rest of human understanding? How much of that needs to be expressed with words or how much of it is just an understanding that does not need to be expressed with words. What are words anyway, sounds in the person's head that mean something or have a definition?

I mean I would need to figure out all of human understanding if I wanted to explain this. That could be a challenging problem that might need to be addressed in another book lol. I don't know how much of what I think is an understanding of some sorts or a verbal understanding that is thought out in a sentence with words.

So we're finally working together. I've explained what a concept is, what logic is, and what understandings are. Sometimes people think with understandings that are non-verbal, while sometimes they think verbally. Theres lots of different subject areas where people need to use concepts and think verbally or think with understandings that are non-verbal.

I remember learning a long time ago that some communication was non-verbal. I mean what is the difference between verbal communication and non-verbal communication? What is thought about that is understood with words versus understood without words? How does that work exactly?

That's kind of complicated, I mean, what does that mean, that sometimes people think with understandings and sometimes they think with words? How does that work out? I could try to follow an analysis or a concept and try to figure out how to explain it, like how the mind works when that concept is being figured out or expressed.

I mean, what mix of understandings, concepts, ideas and words is anything understood? That could be complicated. When anything is figured out it could be verbal or non-verbal, or a mix of both. I'll have to think about that when I try to understand things, whether or not the understanding is verbal or non-verbal, or a mix of the two.

Ok so i'm trying to think here. What exactly do I need to understand. I figured out how the mind works. That's just cognitive psychology, which is about the minds mental processes. The minds mental processes are perception, memory, emotion, language, deciding, thinking and reasoning and attention,
So I know how all of that works, i can think clearly so what else am I missing? If I am thinking clearly then there's nothing else I need to do I don't think. I mean thinking clearly is the main goal in life. If i can think clearly then i can have a lot of emotions and stuff and still function. If i can function then what else would i need to do.
If i can function then what else would I need to do.

I mean if i'm functioning then i'm doing perfectly fine, I can think clearly which i now realize is rather a simple task. Sometimes emotions make thinking clearly more challenging, however, but I think I am prepared for that.

So i can think perfectly clearly, that's what the goal is. I had to learn a lot in order to understand how the mind works. That way I can be more conscious of what I am thinking. I've always been a clear thinker, however my mind has become much more developed over the years and it has become more complicated to think clearly.

I mean, like when I was a child I would have emotions but not be aware those emotions were occurring, I guess I was aware I was having the emotions but now I'm a lot more conscious of my emotions.

Before I didn't even understand what emotion regulation was. Now I understand that emotion regulation is the attempt of the mind to control its own emotions and maintain them. I've become a more conscious person over the years, so i know when i'm thinking or when i'm having an emotion. As a child I could think and have emotions, but I was not aware that that was happening, well I guess I knew it was happening but wasn't as aware of how my mind was working as I am now.

Now I have emotions and thoughts, but I am aware that I am having emotions and thoughts. Like I am clear thinking. WHen i have an emotion, I am aware that I am having that emotion, and when I have a thought, I am aware that I am having that thought. That's all part of thinking clearly.

So what do I need to know in order to think clearly, that's the important question. Do I need to know anything about critical thinking or logic?

I mean, what do i need to know about logic in order to think clearly. I know that I think with language and with words and that words are sounds in the head. I also know that there are standards for critical thinking, like accuracy and proficiency. In order to be a critical thinker accuracy is one of the standards. THeres also validity, how truthful something is. I mean i'm thinking clearly right now and there isn't much going on in my head. When an emotion comes I just observe the emotion. WHen a thought comes I also observe the thought and remain clear thinking.

So what have I memorized that helps me think clearly, I've memorized the 6 mental processes of memory, attention, perception, thinking, deciding and reasoning, emotion and language.

I've also memorized the critical thinking skills of accuracy and validity. Validity is how truthful something is, is that statement valid, and accuracy is how accurate it is, which is similar to how valid it is.

I also know that there is emotion and cognition, the relationship between emotion and cognition, and that people can make appraisals of their emotional state. The appraisal is cognitive, while it assesses the persons emotions, or is about their emotions.

What else have I learned? I've learned that there are primary emotions that are more important than the other emotions, the primary emotions are happy, sad, anger, fear, surprise and disgust. There's also love and hate but i don't think those are primary emotions, they're strong emotions, but the primary emotions are supposed to have a facial expression which is physiological.

What else have I learned, there's other emotions that i don't remember the names of but those aren't primary emotions. I see why happy and sad are primary emotions and I also can see why anger and fear are primary emotions. I would think that surprise and disgust aren't as important as the other 4 primary emotions, those seem more short-lived.

What else have I learned? I've learned that consciousness is the sum total of our mental processes, and that there is an ego which is unconscious or an unconscious drive of our own identity that wants us to succeed, and that if we are conscious of our ego it doesn't exist anymore because its conscious and under our control and no longer and unconscious drive, but a conscious one.

What else have I learned. I've learned that the difference between feelings and emotions is that emotions are stronger than feelings and can be more intellectual, especially more intellectual than the physical sensations or feelings, the physical sensationa like cold and warm are kind of stupid feelings, while emotions can be more intellectual because they are stronger and more mental than the physical feelings.

What else have I learned? I've learned that there's categorization of ideas and objects, and if you list the objects or ideas there's only a limited number of them.

I've also learned about CBT, or cognitive behavioral therapy which tries to track if someone is experiencing an emotion, thought or behavior and how those three are linked or occur, which one occurs first and does it lead to another one, like does the emotion lead to a thought which then could lead to a behavior.

Um, so what else have I learned. All those things are important if I want to think clearly.

I've also learned that some feelings can be more intellectual than other feelings, like I pointed out that emotions can be more intellectual than feelings because they are deeper or more powerful, that might make them more intellectual.

Um, so what have I learned again, I mentioned CBT or cognitive behavioral therapy, the difference between emotions and feelings, the mental processes, cognitive appraisals of our emotional states, logic and accuracy and validity of statements or thoughts, that language is sound in our heads, what else have I learned here that i might need to know.

I can break it down based upon the mental processes I already listed. For instance the mental process of perception could involve visual or conceptual information, for example everything is visual when you first see it, then some of the objects become concepts in your head that you can think about in addition to your ordinary thinking with language.

The mental process of memory can include thinking about stuff that happened in the past, and enables you to think about multiple things at once (that is, pull up an idea from memory at the same time as thinking about or coming up with a new idea at the same time).

The mental process of emotion means that people have emotions, and that they can be combined with thoughts that the person could think about. I've already mentioned that people can make appraisals of their emotional states. The appraisal is cognitive while it's about your feelings, or your emotions.

There's more to say about perceptual things in your vision and conceptual information in your head, people think with concepts that are important while at the same time thinking about visual information or what they are seeing. I mean how does that work, there is a steady stream of thought while the person is looking at things, that seems kind of simple. The visual could cause the person to think of new things, or they could be using their memory.

There's also analytical reasoning. But I mean what does someone need to know about that, that is also pretty simple. For any argument or statement, or concept there is how truthful it is. Is that statement accurate or true. You could ask yourself that for each statement that you make. Since people think with words in their heads, then it makes sense that they can check if the sentences they think with are valid statements and if they are accurate.

But I mean, is it really that simple, for a person to keep track of everything they are thinking and then check to see if what they are thinking is accurate and valid (truthful).

If you think about it, everything someone thinks can be checked to see if it's valid. That was part of the observing mind, when I have a thought, I observe the thought to see what I am thinking, and then I can check to see if the thought makes sense. I can also do the same thing with my emotions.

Now what else would there be to thinking logically other than keeping track of all of your thoughts and emotions and observing them logically. If I am doing that, then it would seem like I have all of the logic figured out I would say.

What else could be going on inside the mind then. I already mentioned that there is perception and cognition, when someone sees an object they think about it in their mind, that shows how perception is related to cognition. That's important to know, though it seems kind of obvious. I mean obviously someone looks at things and then thinks about those things. That's a primary function of the mind if you think about it.

What else is going on then in the mind, there's a steady visual and then the person thinks about what they just saw. They can also think about other things other than things they pull up from their environment. I mean they could use their memory to recall other objects or other ideas that they could think about.

So that means either someone is thinking about something that immediately relates to what they are doing or that indirectly relates to what they are doing, that seems rather obvious. I'm trying to observe what Is going on in my head most of the time. I mean i'm in my room typing on my computer right now so I also notice the activity that I am doing.

What else would someone need to notice. That seems like basic logic right? I mean I'm just working step by step here, I think about things that I'm doing that are immediately obvious like what I am doing, and what is going on around me. I also have the television on which I occasionally glance at, that's something else that I've been doing.

That means that people can keep track of their actions, its good to know that so they can be more aware or conscious of what they are doing. I don't know why that didn't occur to me before, I mean before I was doing actions but didn't notice that I was doing them, well I knew I was doing those actions but I didn't think to myself 'well now I am doing this action'.

I mean, people have to know what they are doing, are they seeing things or are they thinking about stuff? That's an interesting question, I mean most of what people do is either see with their visual eyes or their mental perception, or they think about stuff that is going on in their head. They could be thinking about the emotions that they are feeling, or they could be thinking about the thoughts that they are thinking. The question is, are they aware of everything they are doing? I guess there is sort of 'awareness of their awareness' that is occurring. I mean, do they know everything that is going on in their heads?

What could be going on in their heads then? They could be experiencing emotions, or they could be thinking about things. They are also doing stuff in their immediate environment.

An Overview of my research
And biography
By Mark Rozen Pettinelli
Online handle – xiornik
2020

https://drive.google.com/folderview?id=1kiGfJRhyz8Cre-qJR6lkCSSXhxiKR4-gm

Ok so I've been doing my own research since I graduated from concord academy in 2003. I was meeting with therapists and got

put on a lot of medication, I guess that my research on cognitive psychology mixed with their understanding of people and their emotions as therapists. I tried to make my research practical, finding only the important information and the information that was relevant to myself, like managing my own emotions and thoughts. I don't know what my therapists were thinking about my analysis but they have their own more practical understanding, or an understanding that applies to other people who have different emotions from me. I'm kind of unique but have been meeting with the autism network people for almost 2 years now (in addition to interacting with the staff in my group home and meeting with other therapists).

So what did I learn? I bought a bunch of cognitive psychology books and went through those over the past decade. Now it's the end of 2020 and I wrote my psychology of emotions, feelings and thoughts book at the end of 2006.

So what am I supposed to learn from these books? I already wrote a lot of information about feelings and thoughts in my previous articles. I know the difference between an emotion and a feeling, I wrote about that. Again, a feeling is something you feel, that is why the word 'feel' is used, and emotions are supposed to be strong feelings, like the primary emotions.

I don't know if each person responds to stimuli with a primary emotion first, I would think that the emotions could come in any order.

So any feeling could occur at any time, in any order.

I'm writing this article for my own sake, so i can understand my feelings and thoughts more. And understand how my mind works.

The words 'emotion' and 'feeling' can be used interchangeably, except emotions are supposed to be stronger than feelings. That is why there are only 6 primary emotions of happy, sad, anger, fear, surprise and disgust. Those primary emotions are more powerful or more 'main' than the other feelings humans can experience.

The list of books in this article I think have interesting titles that I could benefit from if the books actually have good information.

What or how do feelings work in the mind? That is the question. Like right now what am I feeling? Those are interesting questions. Do some feelings always come first or do feelings occur in any order?

There are many feelings that people can experience, it's kind of interesting actually. Sometimes feelings are strong, and sometimes they are weak, and sometimes they are mostly unconscious.

I don't really know which feelings I have first or even have period. Maybe I just have a simple mind I guess.

If I have a simple mind, then I should be able to keep track of which feelings I have, when they come and go, if they are unconscious or conscious, and also what my thoughts are.

Thoughts are more intellectual than feelings, and feelings can be physical or emotional, or even intellectual feelings. That is like what I said before, that thought or some feelings can feel or be more intellectual. Some feelings might be stupid also, like some of the stupid physical bodily sensations.

I have about 5 different cognitive psychology textbooks in my room that i've been going through for at least a couple of years now. I also have some other books about psychology and other topics I was interested in, like the topic of emotion and cognition.

I'm going to go through more books that I've just got recently, however I just started going through those books.

These are two of the cognitive psychology books i've been going through:

Cognitive Psychology: A Student's Handbook 7th Edition

- by Michael W. Eysenck (Author), Mark T. Keane (Author)

How is it that noticing if something is living that a conceptual thing? Some things like perceptual features, like what it looks like, is clearly perceptual priming. This means that either something is visual or it is conceptual. What is the difference? I mean the mind can think with images that it 'sees' and it can think with concepts that it thinks about. It also has a continuous stream of visual information if their eyes are open anyway. Conceptual information could be just things that a person is thinking about.

"Judgement involves deciding on the likelihood of various events"

The statement about judgement is a little bit confusing, how could there be a partial understanding of anything? Judgement means the person uses accuracy to come to a conclusion from a guess or a measured assessment. That's kind of like the scientific method, the person weighs evidence and comes to a conclusion they think is correct. Decision making is also part of that process because they have to decide about how to go about coming to or arriving at the proper conclusion.

The mind isn't that complicated, language is fairly simple, thinking is fairly simple, and so are feelings and emotions. Appraisals of our emotional states can influence the emotions involved, that is also a simple thing to understand. Cognition and emotion are connected that way - humans think about things that influence their emotions and their feelings, in turn, influence what the person is thinking about.

I mean, how complicated can language be? Language is just words that signify something in the mind, and sentences are more complicated than a simple word by itself. A sentence is more complicated than one word. Take the word 'dog', the word dog is a noun that could be the subject of a sentence, so the dog could be doing something - some action that is described with a verb in the sentence, say the sentence 'the dog is running' has one subject, the dog, and one verb 'running'. That is an example of a typical sentence with a subject that is performing an action, the action is the verb in the sentence, and the subject of the sentence is the dog who is doing the action.

Language is simple like that, however only the human species has the ability to use language.

This book helped me realize how simple the mind is. There is consciousness, which consists of humans observing their environment, thinking consciously about their emotions and thoughts, thinking with language and turning sounds into speech in their head (a process called lexicalisation), and just responding to their environment.

How complicated is that? I can keep track of most of what is going on in my head, I have language and speech that I use and words I think to myself to help me keep track of what is going on in my head. I also use speech to communicate with other people, but that is fairly simple, I mean, things like saying 'hello' and 'how are you' are fairly simple to understand.

I might not know how to communicate in other languages other than english (I remember a few basic words in spanish (which i took in high school)) but there are probably equivalent words in other languages for each word or phrase in the english language.

So what else does the mind do that's too complicated? There's a section on emotion and cognition in the book, a section on consciousness, a section on judgement and decision making. All those seem like simple concepts or topics. Even the section on speech and language. Also the chapter on problem solving is fairly simple.

Cognitive psychology is supposed to cover the mind's mental processes and this book discusses all of them, however there aren't that many mental processes that the mind uses or thinks about to itself. That makes the mind a fairly simple organ. I mean, I'm sure the details of neuroscience get pretty complicated, but when you look at the mind from the perspective of cognitive psychology then there is only a few processes going on at any time.

- The Oxford Handbook of Cognitive Psychology (Oxford Library of Psychology)

By Daniel Reisberg
So i think that means that implicit memory can effect a person because they have memories in their mind but they don't know that those had an impact on them, however they still helped shape the person and therefore have an impact on them.

What does that exactly mean? If there is an input representation, then your mind is going to see the input some way initially, either if this is a visual image or a representation of the visual they see. That makes sense, humans see visuals all the time, and it stays in their memory for a while, and it can be modified so they can remember the visual in their mind by simplifying the visual with a representation of the visual.

"Beliefs are about something"
That makes perfectly good sense, humans can have beliefs, however they are going to be about something and they're going to be formed somehow. How do people form their beliefs? Do they see objects in the real world and then form opinions? Or do they think internally and form beliefs based off of their own analysis?

Here is a list of books I have that I went through:

Master Your Emotions: A Practical Guide to Overcome Negativity and Better Manage Your Feelings (Mastery Series Book 1)

by Thibaut Meurisse (Author)

What is 'the ego'? The book says it's your self identity that you've constructed throughout your lifetime, however I would just call that your 'unconscious' self. I mean your own self identity is going to need to have an important place in your mind, so it would be unconscious, and it would need to have power, like the unconscious mind has power. I also said before that most of the mind is conscious, so the ego would also be unconscious.

The book says that the 'ego and awareness cannot coexist" because as your awareness increases, your ego disappears. That's because your ego is your identity, if you are aware of your identity then you don't need an unconscious one. I would say that works for most things, as the unconscious mind becomes conscious, the unconscious aspects begin to disappear because they become conscious instead.

The ego clings to tons of things to make itself stronger like beliefs, attachments and items. So this means that I think the ego is like your unconscious self, constantly working for you only unconsciously instead of deliberate, conscious actions and thoughts.

The ego wants you to strive to be a better person and achieve stuff in life. That makes sense because your ego is like your unconscious mind, and humans are naturally selfish beings.

The book also states that 'emotions come and go'. That is important to understand because you might want to control your emotions, so it might be good to know when they are occurring.

It also states that negative emotions can be useful. I think that I'd rather not have any negative emotions at all, or maybe just an insignificant amount of them if they're needed to contrast strong, happy emotions.

The book says that emotions can be reinforced by your thinking. For instance negative emotions could be thought about and made stronger, or positive emotions could be thought about and reinforced. Feelings and thoughts become emotions when you think about them. An emotion by itself is weak unless you identify with it. I think that's what the book was trying to explain.

That means that your interpretation of your own emotions is important. That makes sense, I mean if you think about it feelings by themselves have to be interpreted by your conscious mind - that gives you some control over your own emotions because you can choose how you respond to or make your own feelings and thoughts.

The book also states that "interpretation, identification and repetition" of emotions will make them stronger. That makes sense, emotions can be changed by your conscious mind. People can repeat emotions, identify with them, or interpret them in a certain way. I mean if you think about it you can have a lot of conscious control over your emotions by either interpreting your emotions differently, or identifying with them differently.

I don't know what exactly to do to change my own emotions, I know that I can think about which emotions I am experiencing and see if I can change my interpretations of those emotions and see if that works.

I mean, how are you supposed to control your own emotions? The book suggests that you can think about your emotions in order to change them through identification, interpretation, and repetition.

It is harder than that though I would think in order to change your emotions. It's important to understand that the conscious mind interprets feelings and thoughts a certain way, and your interpretation can change how you feel, understand, and experience your emotions.

I mean it's like you have a conscious mind and an unconscious mind, and in order to conceptualize or interpret your feelings you have to think and understand.

Otherwise your feelings could just stay unconscious or unfiltered.

Master Your Thinking: A Practical Guide to Align Yourself with Reality and Achieve Tangible Results in the Real World (Mastery Series Book 5)

by Thibaut Meurisse (Author)

This book suggests that our current thinking is inaccurate. People tend to think with biases and make assumptions. If we align ourselves with reality we can control our thinking and be more productive. I don't know how someone is supposed to think more positively if life is hard though. I've resorted to being delusional and that makes me happy. The book suggests we should think realistically but positively. I don't know how to think positively if life is so hard and difficult, I would think the only way out is to be delusional.

Maybe controlling our thoughts could help us think more realistically, but that doesn't change the fact that life is hard and that it's hard to achieve success in life. I mean, if people are biased and make assumptions that's fine, but how are they supposed to be positive in a hard, unrealistic (I mean difficult) world? It's hard to align yourself with reality if reality is hard, the book doesn't really address that.

The Contemplative Brain: Meditation, Phenomenology and Self-Discovery from a Neuroanthropological Point of View Paperback – October 10, 2020

by Charles D Laughlin (Author)

That's kind of interesting, he lists 4 different states of consciousness there, obviously awake and sleeping are two different states of consciousness. Also dizzy or tipsy is a state of consciousness that doesn't have to be made just by drinking alcohol. Someone could get dizzy because they are tired for instance. I don't know all the conditions that could make someone hallucinate.

The main conscious state would just be 'awake' and 'here'. That would mean that the person is conscious and functioning properly. I don't know how someone could go into a dream state without actually falling asleep, however. I would think that different experiences influence our state of consciousness all the time, depending on the experience. Sometimes an experience could make the person dizzy, I suppose. More or less awake could happen often to a person also.

The Happiness Trap: How to Stop Struggling and Start Living: A Guide to ACT Paperback – Illustrated, June 3, 2008

by Russ Harris (Author), Steven C. Hayes PhD (Foreword)

What is the 'observing self'? It's kind of like an inner eye. In the book it says it could be comparable to the sky, and our feelings are the weather and the rain and the wind. The observing self I would say is like an inner eye, it sees and observes what is going on, but does it respond, because it is just like an eye that cannot be touched.

So it could use an acceptance strategy because it just observes, but would be unable to use a control strategy because that would require intervention.

So an acceptance strategy could use the observing self, observing your feelings and thoughts but not intervening.

Here are books that I got after the others and read

The Oxford Handbook of the Philosophy of Consciousness

by Uriah Kriegel (Editor)

This book states that after the philosophy of consciousness finishes explaining consciousness a 'science of consciousness' will take its place. I don't know what that could mean for all of the explaining. What would it take for consciousness to be fully explained? After the speculation is done by the philosophers it would become a sort of 'science of consciousness'.

They need to reframe 'how to explain' to 'what needs explaining'. If you think about it that makes sense, the conscious phenomena, or the observed facts about consciousness, need to be explained somehow, and it needs to be outlined what exactly needs explanation.

Psychology tries to explain behavioral phenomena, and the study or science of consciousness should try to explain consciousness. How are conscious phenomena supposed to be explained?

There's the experience of conscious thought for instance, what is it to think about something? Is that an experience of consciousness?

I talk about important aspects of consciousness in this article, I mention that thoughts and emotions can be either conscious, unconscious, or semi-conscious. Also that you can reinforce unconscious thoughts and emotions by thinking about them or filtering them so they can become more conscious and under your control. That applies to both thoughts and emotions.

Is consciousness just the 'sum total of its psychological functions'? As mentioned in the book, I mean, how does consciousness arise? It would seem that it is just the 'sum total of its psychological functions'. I would say that's a perfectly fine description of how consciousness arises and what it is. I've already pointed out in this article that there are only a few mental processes going on at any moment, like perception, emotion, attention, memory, language, deciding, thinking and reasoning. Those mental processes combined are everything that is going on in the brain, and give rise to consciousness.

I listed those mental processes but I didn't include 'introspection', which could account for internal thinking. Thinking was listed as a mental process, but more can be said about thought other than that the person is thinking. The person could be regulating their emotions, for instance making their emotions stronger or interpreting their unconscious emotions and making them conscious. That function involves the two mental processes of both thinking and emotion.

What else could a person think about through introspection? I mean they do more than regulate their own emotions and thoughts, which is self-regulation and emotion regulation. Self regulation could include regulating their own thoughts, goals, problem solving and planning and is similar to or includes executive functioning. Executive functioning is self regulating your own mind by using your thoughts I would say. While emotion regulation is just regulating your own emotions, both of which could be done through introspective thought.

I mean, what exactly is executive functioning or self-regulation? I would think it is using your own thoughts or power of introspection to monitor your own mind, your own thoughts and your own emotions, while emotion regulation is just handling your emotions.

Also, part of self-regulation is monitoring your own attention (not just your thoughts), which was another mental process that I mentioned. How does controlling your own attention give rise to consciousness? How conscious the person is relates and is partially determined by their attention and what they are paying attention to, that seems kind of obvious.

The book also states that "conscious states are states we're aware of". That seems rather obvious, considering that the definition of conscious is "aware".

The Oxford Handbook of Rationality (Oxford Handbooks)

by Alfred R. Mele (Editor), Piers Rawling (Editor)

"Reasoning is a process that can modify intentions and beliefs."

There's also a difference between "what to believe" and "what to intend to do". People also have "practical reasons to believe something". Does someone allow arbitrary decisions or have wishful thinking? I already pointed out that there is a more type of unconscious type of thinking, that is more arbitrary or without the use of reasoning. Unconscious thought is more illogical and arbitrary and can bypass working memory, while conscious thought is more intentional and uses more reasoning.

There's also a relationship between reasoning and rationality. People have an "account of what it is for beliefs and desires to be justified". "Kant: Rationality as Practical Reason".

Fear is a thought that some anticipated judgement poses a threat. Is there an appropriateness of an emotional response? Emotion is a threat to rationality, however long term they might help the decision of rational options over time. There are factors leading to action, an affective state can modify the person's practical options. I suppose that means that the person needs to take initiative and monitor or figure out their emotional state in order to make practical decisions.

There's also "motivationally biased belief" "Motivationally biased believers test hypotheses and believe on the basis of evidence." But there is still the influence of motivation to be considered.

Also, "what is the relationship between rationality and thought", or the "relationship between rationality and language"?

Rationality applies to "actions, beliefs and desires". Also "rational plans, rational views, rational reactions, and rational emotions". People are practical beings seeking to do things, to satisfy our needs and desires.

What is the role of our belief system? Does it accurately represent the world? What is the relationship between beliefs and knowledge? Maybe people can "schieve a rational belief system".

Are our beliefs justified and reasonable?

Perception requires consciousness. Are objects in perception "ideas" in the mind? Or do they become "ideas" in the mind?

"If you see, hear, touch, taste or smell something then it affects you in some way."

Memory is also different from perception. With memory you recall something. You can recall a belief for instance. Can memory help justify a belief? That's an interesting question. Uf it is a source of knowledge then it could be used to justify beliefs.

Consciousness can also be a source of rational belief. Consciousness represents an inner world, There can be objects and representations of them that are 'in' the person's consciousness. A person's inner world can contain sensations, thoughts, numbers and concepts.

Reasoning can be reflection, intuition, and understanding in the mind. When we reflect on a concept, or we can form hypothesis to see what an understanding means or is. There are concepts people can understand after reflection. You could use hypothesis to test understandings and concepts. "We can reason from the "premises" and form conclusions.

Knowledge can use "intuition" which would be guesses that are not guided by information, while there can be guesses that are guided by information, and may include using hypothesis and coming to conclusions.

Does inference need memory? I would think that someone could infer something without using very many details from memory, or is that deductive reasoning? Is a source rationally figured out? There can be rational belief without intuition or deductive reasoning. There can be beliefs and knowledge that doesn't depend on other beliefs, memories or other pieces of knowledge.

Does coherence of understanding need justification? I would think for something to make sense all of the facts would need to fit together. There are different sources of knowledge that all need to make sense. There is also the dependence of a fact on someone's belief system.

A belief system could hold many beliefs, does a person need to go through their own belief system to see if they are believing things that are logical, rational and factual?

There is also the sources of the information for the person's beliefs. Are there ordinary justified beliefs? How does this all work? How far do we need to take a belief in order to justify it or understand it?

The Oxford Handbook of The History of Analytic Philosophy (Oxford Handbooks) 1st Edition

by Michael Beaney (Editor)

Are logical statements dependent on the language that is used? A logical statement could be true is its facts are checked I suppose. Someone could use the scientific method and test hypothesis they form about a fact.

Is intentional action backed by logical thought? If something is intentional then it implies that the person thought about it before performing the action. On the other hand, it could be intentional but not well thought out.

The Oxford Handbook of Philosophy of Mind (Oxford Handbooks) 1st Edition

by Brian McLaughlin (Editor), Ansgar Beckermann (Editor), Sven Walter (Editor)

"What is the content of a perceptual experience?"It depends what it is like for the subject to experience the perceptual experience I suppose.

Also, what is the relationship between thoughts and concepts? Concepts could be fictions, while thoughts are always accurate because it is just a thought. A concept could be inaccurate, illogical or not make sense, while the thought about the concept is more specific.

The Oxford Handbook of Contemporary Phenomenology (Oxford Handbooks in Philosophy) Reprint Edition

by Dan Zahavi (Editor)

What makes color seen as it is? If you think about color it is a perceptual object. Or some object in a person's environment could be a certain color. THat makes perception seem rather simple, that there are just objects in the person's environment that they see that have certain colors.

Does that mean that sense experience has 'conceptual' content? It could just be objects that get represented in the mind, it doesn't need to be logical.

The Oxford Handbook of Thinking and Reasoning (Oxford Library of Psychology)

By Keith J. Holyoak (Editor) and Robert G. Morrison (Editor)

Probabilistic judgement is how people come to conclusions, they weigh certain probabilities and come to a conclusion. People are not computers, however, and their judgements could be biased. I don't know what it would take for someone to always reach logical conclusions.

Furthermore, humans understand concepts at the word level and the sentence level. That means each word has a meaning by itself and a more complicated meaning when it is in a sentence.

"Intuitive judgement" is judgement without using reasoning. So that would be different from judgements that use reasoning. Does that mean that an intuitive judgment is a stupid judgement?

An intuitive judgement could be smart I suppose, if it doesn't require logic to be accurate or intelligent.

Maybe that is like 'deciding from the gut', those types of decisions could be accurate however they don't use logic or reasoning.

People can also use rational judgments to arrive at conclusions. I said that before, it is like they could use something like the scientific method in order to weigh evidence and different options. The scientific method is about weighing evidence and forming and testing theories.

Humans could use a similar way of assessing evidence when judging various options in their decisions or assessments.

It's not like for each conclusion someone comes to the person does some analysis that uses a thorough and rigorous method, like the scientific method.

I mean I don't know what goes on in people's heads each time they go through a process to arrive at a conclusion. I suppose that could be called the decision making process.

Sometimes a person's decision making process could just be intuitive and not use intelligence or a complicated method to reach conclusions, and other times the person might think really hard and use reasoning and logic to figure out a conclusion or solution.

Also there are 2 types of thinking, unconscious thinking and conscious thinking. Unconscious thinking is illogical and can bypass working memory, while conscious thinking is more logical and uses working memory. How can unconscious thought byass working memory? What are all the differences between unconscious thought and conscious thought? I see how conscious thought uses working memory, and maybe if someone is thinking unconsciously then it doesn't need to consciously use working memory, but it might need to unconsciously use working memory.

What does that mean for how people think, however? Working memory is a conscious process that the person uses to think, it is short term and conscious. When the mind thinks unconsciously it doesn't think about working memory but is still influenced by it because it is the unconscious mind.

So the difference between unconscious thinking and conscious thinking then is the difference between the unconscious mind and the conscious mind. Most of the mind is unconscious because humans aren't really in touch with all of their emotions or unconscious thoughts, that makes most of the mind be unconscious.

So unconscious thought is actually the mind thinking unconsciously.

The unconscious mind doesn't really use working memory because that is a conscious process.

I suppose the unconscious mind could influence what a person is thinking about, and that could influence working memory. So the unconscious mind is therefore connected to the conscious mind.

People also think using categories. How exactly does that work, however? I suppose it means that similar objects or ideas are grouped together in the mind. That isn't really a big deal though.

I mean, it's kind of obvious that people would group together similar objects. For instance I grouped together the two different sexes - those are "girls" and those are "boys". But that's part of defining and labeling objects in the mind, in that case, however, they also belong to significant categories.

I suppose that's just how the mind thinks about things, by grouping similar objects and ideas together. It's just association I suppose. For instance when I type on this new computer i'm reminded of all the previous older computers I had over the years. Association and categorization in the mind is a way of learning from similar objects or ideas.

In this book there's a chapter on explanations, which states something like that people constantly search and offer explanations for everything that goes on in their life. I would think that would make people smarter, if they constantly seek to explain and describe what is going on. I don't know everything someone might try to explain, though I would think it could make the person more intelligent and knowledgeable if they have their own inner understanding of the world that they've been trying to explain for years. That's what it's like in my case anyway, I've been offering explanations and analyzing everything for a long time now, it's made me a lot smarter and knowledgeable.

I mean, it's kind of like saying that people have their own internal thinking where they are curious and try to explain the world.

The Blackwell Companion to Consciousness 2nd Edition

by Susan Schneider (Editor), Max Velmans (Editor)

What is self consciousness? Is it just awareness of the self? Or is it awareness of objects that make the self more conscious? How does someone define what the self is? If consciousness is awareness of our own mental states, then how does that give rise to self-consciousness? I suppose that if a person is aware of their own mental state then they are self-conscious. What could their mental state be in that circumstance? If a human knows if he is conscious and awake then they know if they are conscious.

As a kid I didn't understand that I was conscious, I just had simple thoughts. I mean I suppose I knew that I was alive, but I didn't say to myself, "I am conscious, I think about stuff and have thoughts, I am aware of my environment and my own conscious state". I just didn't think about myself that way. Now I can label myself as being conscious and alive, where before as a child I might have just understood that I was alive.

Being conscious involves understanding that you are conscious, i have feelings and thoughts all of the time, and as a conscious person understand that those feelings and thoughts help make me conscious. When I was a child I would have feelings and thoughts, however I did not reflect upon them or try to control them to a greater extent.

Conclusion:

So I'm trying to figure out if that's all the information I need to know to function in life. In previous books I wrote more about feelings and consciousness, however this is my final book.

I mean, if I can keep track of my feelings and thoughts, and understand the basic mental processes like thought, language, perception, decision making, emotion, attention, and reasoning then I would think i know everything I would need to know.

I can also keep track of my feelings and know the difference between feelings and emotions to help me sort them out. For instance there are only 6 basic emotions that have physiological correlates of facial expressions they are happy, sad, anger, fear, surprise and disgust.

Other feelings that are strong could also be considered to be emotions because one definition of emotion is "any strong feeling" like a strong feeling of love could be considered an emotion but it wouldn't be one of the basic emotions.

Also, in order to keep track of my feelings I need to know that feelings could be the result of the primary emotions, or the conscious experience of the primary emotions.

But there are many feelings that could be independent of the primary emotions I think like hopeless or edgy or self-loving. Those could be experienced any time and be largely independent of the primary emotions, or they could be the conscious experience of feelings of those primary emotions.

That's useful to know if you want to keep track of your feelings, emotions or thoughts.

The information in this book is also useful to know, I talk about and review information about consciousness, judgement and decision making, cognition and emotion, and other topics related to cognition or psychology.

What else would be needed in order to further the research field, like what am I studying here. A cognitive scientist probably knows all of that stuff about the brain and how feelings and thoughts work in the brain, and so would a cognitive psychologist except they might not know how it works in the brain. Also clearly neuroscientists and neurologists know that kind of stuff.

There's also therapists and psychiatrists, i don't know the difference between what all those different professions learn about emotions and feelings. I'm trying to progress the research field here lol.

I've explained my analysis of feelings and emotions and thoughts enough times. Feelings can feel intellectual or that might be when they are more conscious, and there are the primary emotions which are facial expressions. I don't know how much more important the main emotions are from the other feelings someone can experience.

I wrote before that a feeling might not be intense but be clear to you, or it could be clear to you but not intense.

I mean i'm trying to advance the research field here but don't know what all those professions and professionals already know about feelings and thoughts, I'm offering my interpretation and explanation. I mean therapists must have known a lot of stuff about feelings a long time ago.

I've tried to keep my analysis practical and only absorb or figure out the important information I would need for myself. Therapists also must have a practical analysis because they have to help people manage their feelings and thoughts. I've been meeting with therapists and nurses for a long time now.

Further Conclusion:

So what else would need to be explored other than what is in this article? I have another article where I talk about how feelings can feel intellectual or be stupid feelings, like the stuipid physical sensations. If a feeling is intellectual does that mean it's more like an emotion or thought? Emotions are deep and powerful, so they could be more like thoughts.

Or is that just describing what feelings feel like? That they could feel different ways, intellectual, stupid, conscious, unconscious, powerful, weak, etc.

What are all the ways I can describe what feelings feel like then? There are the mental processes like perception, attention, emotions, language, and reasoning. Part of the mental process of emotion involves experiencing feelings.

Feelings can feel tons of different ways. There are different mental states and states of consciousness, for instance. If a person is conscious of their mental states they could become more conscious, or more self-conscious.

Furthermore, if people can think about any idea or concept, then there is a lot they can think about. I mean, cognitive science would call that idea in their head an idea that they haven't figured out yet or that is incomplete.

So what kinds of ideas could people be thinking about that they need to think more about? I don't know the answer to that. I feel like I know everything with my knowledge of how the brain works and cognitive science. For instance it is important to know the difference between emotions and feelings so you can keep track of your own feelings and emotions.

Once again, one definition of emotion could be "any strong feeling", also there are only 6 primary emotions of anger, happy, sad, fear, surprise and disgust. Those emotions are more primary than the other emotions someone might be feeling like if love is a strong feeling it could be considered to be an emotion.

It's also important to point out that primary emotions usually come first because they have physiological facial expressions as bodily reactions. Then feelings are felt as the conscious reaction to those primary emotions.

On the other hand, it seems like feelings and emotions could occur in any order. So if I know how to keep track of my emotions and feelings then I am on top of my mental state and know what I am doing. I also could know how conscious I am - for instance I said before that as a kid I just knew I was alive and didn't know how conscious or aware I was. Now I know what my feelings are, what my thoughts are, and mostly what my mental state is. That's all a part of being conscious and aware.

Enough Information

Well, that seems like it's enough information to know in order to function in life. The information about feelings helps people keep track of their feelings. And the information about consciousness and thoughts helps people keep track of their self-awareness and their thoughts at any moment.

What else would someone need to know? It's important to know that there is unconscious thought and conscious thought. For instance your unconscious ego could be making decisions for you or motivating you in general without you being aware of it. Your ego wants you to be successful, it is an unconscious drive of your own consciousness, or your own self-identity that drives you.

What else is important about unconscious thought? People might be feeling emotions and feelings that they are not aware of, those feelings could be motivating them to act or making them feel different ways that could help them or hurt them, depending on the emotion. If they understand what they are feeling, then perhaps they can filter the emotion or change it to something they want to experience.

I suppose that's all I need to know in order to function in life. I know I have unconscious emotions and unconscious thoughts, that should help me be more conscious and in control of my emotions and thoughts.

I also know about the different things I talked about in this article - such as that thoughts can be unconscious, that there are primary emotions and more minor feelings, that I can be more self-conscious of my mental states or just more conscious in general, that I can use rational or instinctive judgements (a rational judgement is more conscious than an instinctive judgement, which would be more unconscious or automatic).

What else would I need to know, the information in this article seems important, it talks about feelings, thoughts, consciousness, mental states, controlling feelings and thoughts, and visual and perceptual and conceptual information, and judgement and decision making.

More on the Emotions and Feelings "hoffman - "feelings list""

So I've already said that there are 6 main emotions of happy, sad, anger, fear, surprise and disgust. But what makes those emotions the main emotions? They are more powerful so they all have facial expressions I think. They are the emotions people usually feel, while other feelings are just other ways of feeling. There are many feelings that fall under the category of the 'happy' emotion, like amazed, delighted, invigorated, satisfied and thrilled. There are also other emotions that fall under the categories of the other emotions. For instance sad could be anguished, depressed, disappointed, discouraged, heartbroken, lonely, unhappy, etc. There are also feelings that are part of the angry emotion such as aggravated, edgy, furious, hostile, impatient, moody, outraged, and upset. These are some feelings that are part of the emotion 'fear' -

afraid, frightened, nervous, panic, scared, terrified and worried. There are also other feelings people can experience such as accepting/open, courageous/powerful, connected/loving, disconnected/numb, embarrassed/shame, guilt, hopeful, powerfless, tender, stressed/tense, and unsettled/doubt.

Those are all ways of feeling. I pointed out that there are the 6 primary emotions, and then other ways of feeling things. The question is, what makes the primary emotions more powerful or more 'main' emotions? Is it that they are felt first and have physiological facial expressions? The other feelings are just ways of feeling and are secondary to the primary emotions. For instance loving is second to the emotion of 'happy'. Guilty is secondary to the emotion of 'fear'. There are also the feelings that fall under the same category as the primary emotions, which I already pointed out. There's also the bodily sensations, like achy, cold, full, flowing, empty, sore, or throbbing. Those are more stupid and are just physical sensations, and aren't secondary to the primary emotions like the other mental feelings are.

Final Analysis

Ok, so i think that's all the information I need to know. The final two sections of this paper I filled out were the two books of rationality and analytic philosophy. Now the question is, what else do I need to know?

I've already discussed the basics of rationality, such as that there could be a belief system that needs to be checked. Are all of someone's beliefs rational? How does rationality contribute to consciousness?

Its true, most of our conscious mind contains memories, sensations, thoughts, and other mental entities that contribute to our self-consciousness. There's also various different mental states that a person can be in.

Thinking about the statement in the book on phenomenology, are perceptions of objects conceptual in the mind? What is the relationship between perception and thought?

How does an object become represented in the mind, or what are all the things someone could be thinking about?

That goes back to the statement I made before, that consciousness is the sum total of our mental processes. One of our mental processes is vision, we see the objects in our environment and they become concepts or objects in our mind.

The other mental processes also become part of our conscious mind, like emotion and attention are two important mental processes. All the different processes of the mind contribute to the person's self-consciousness, including the objects they see in their environment.

The important question I have to ask is - what is the information that any person would need to know in order to function in society? I would think that they would need a basic understanding of emotions and thoughts. Cognitive Behavioral Therapy - or CBT for short is a practice of therapy where the patient tracks his or her emotions, thoughts and actions. That is, how their emotions and feelings lead to thoughts and how their thoughts lead actions. That also would obviously include how external actions also lead to the persons internal feelings and thoughts. Its kind of obvious that the analysis of keeping track of how feelings lead to thoughts and thoughts lead to feelings, and how thoughts and feelings lead to actions - is important. I would think that a person would need to keep track of their own feelings and actions and that would be important for the person. I mean everyone would want to know what they are feeling at any moment. Also what feelings lead to which thoughts and which thoughts lead to feelings. They could also keep track of how actions in the external world lead to their own internal emotions and thoughts. So in terms of what information would be important for someone to know I would think understanding how to keep track of their own emotions and thoughts would be an important thing for the person to understand. Another thing to understand would be what the difference between emotions and feelings is. Anything could be a feeling since the definition of the word is 'feel'. Emotions are theoretically any strong feeling. Does that mean that the sensation of 'cold' could be an emotion? If someone has a tactile feeling of cold when they touch something does that mean it could be an emotion if it becomes a stronger feeling or sensation of 'cold' ? Or are emotions few and basic emotions, like happy or sad or anger or surprise. Those are part of the few dened basic emotions. What is the difference between emotions and feelings then? A feeling is anything you can feel while emotions are deep and primary, there is only a few of them. Feelings can be sensations of anything that is tactile or that you can feel.

1.1 Other Important things in life

What would be other important information for a person to know about in life? I mean   what else do I know as part of my background knowledge or knowledge that I use. I have a high school education and took a few college courses. High school educations are extremely important - they teach basic sciences, algebra, English language, possibly foreign language also and maybe history. I studied my emotions and thoughts and the study of consciousness after I graduated from high school because I was put on medications and met with therapists. Cognitive psychology was also another topic that I studied - or just basic psychology and maybe cognition or the study of thinking. Is that a complete explanation of what I know? A description of a high school education and then my self studies after high school? I mean consciousness is a dicult topic to study. Thankfully the medications I was on helped me to study my own consciousness and how I think and feel and experience the world. I mean, what else would be important for someone to know? If they know what they are feeling at any one time, then they have a good idea as to what is going on. If they also know their thoughts and how their thoughts relate to their feelings, then they have a good idea of what they are feeling and thinking at any moment. That is probably more important than other things they could focus on. So what else could someone be doing? There are tons of different types of experience someone could have or activities they could be doing at any given time. Its important to know that they can focus on their internal feelings, or think with thoughts, or do certain actions or observe or partake in certain external actions or activities.

1.2 Actions and Emotions

So then it's just a matter of what action or activity or experience someone is engaged in. There are dierent feelings for any action or activity someone could be doing. That means that humans have thoughts and emotions. Feeling'. Emotion could mean 'any strong However there are only a few basic emotions such as happy or sad or anger or surprise. Those are primary emotions. What are all the complicated feelings someone could experience? There's a lot of feelings for sure, however some of these feelings are physical sensations, while other feelings are more intellectual or deep like love or caring. That means that emotions can be intellectual, if you think about it there are intellectual feelings like thoughts could be considered to be intellectual feelings. A thought is dierent from a feeling because it is more intellectual, that means that feels more intellectual while a feeling might be more stupid or more like a sensation. Can I explore that idea further? There are physical actions that could cause basic physical sensations or feelings like when someone engages in hard physical work. Those would probably lead to physical sensations. If someone is thinking about information it might lead to intellectual stimulation or a feeling of intelligence.

1.3 Emotions, Feelings and Thoughts

Maybe I should go into more detail about the difference between feelings and thoughts, and the difference between emotions and feelings. I've already said that thoughts can feel intellectual. Feelings could feel stupid or physical, however. An emotion, however, could be any strong feeling. That means that the feeling of cold when go out on a cold day, go into cold water or just touch something cold could be considered an emotion if it is a strong feeling of cold. I would dene that as just a strong feeling however, not like a primary emotion of fear, anger, surprise, or happy or sad. Those emotions are more intellectual than just a sensation of 'cold'. What is the difference between all of the feelings someone can experience then? A feeling could be happy or sad, or anger or surprise right. That means that there are a huge number of feelings that someone can experience. There are also intellectual thoughts that someone could have. I thought that a feeling or emotion like love would be more deep and intellectual than the feeling or sensation of cold - like when you touch something that is cold it is just a sensation. So what is the difference between all of the different feelings and emotions that someone could experience? Some feelings i think could be more intellectual, while other feelings are more like sensations or things you can touch that are tactile.

That brings up a lot more questions about what feelings are like and what emotions are like. I said already that a feeling could feel more stupid like the feeling of cold or a simple physical sensation. There are also more deep intellectual feelings someone could experience. Those are all interesting questions. I think some feelings can be more intellectual or deep while other feelings could be more stupid and powerful. The question then is - what is the difference between all the feelings that someone could experience? There are thoughts, and then there are basic feelings which are different from thoughts. Thoughts are intellectual, while feelings are physical or simple. Are feelings just simple thoughts then? Or is a feeling anything that is physical? A thought could be connected to a physical feeling, however, in terms of a chain of events of a thought leading to a feeling or a feeling leading to a thought.

1.4 Clarication of feelings

There needs to be a clarification here, what then exactly is the difference between thoughts and feelings? I already pointed out that there could be a difference between feelings and emotions, emotions could be deeper and more like how thoughts are intellectual, while feelings could be more like stupid physical sensations.

Does that mean that there could be a stupid thought? Could there a be an intelligent feeling or a stupid feeling? I know that there could be a powerful feeling like the feeling of cold when someone goes into cold water, that could be a powerful feeling of cold, for instance. What would be an example of a powerful intellectual feeling then? Are there even powerful thoughts? How could a thought even be powerful? I understand how a feeling could be powerful because of physical work and exercise. Those are obviously powerful physical feelings.

However, how then could a thought be powerful if it is just intellectual? Anxiety could be like a powerful intellectual feeling because anxiety is somewhat separate from stupid physical feelings, making it more like an intellectual thought.

1.5 Some Notes

How could a person's emotions and feelings, and of course their thoughts, be described? Is it a simple task to track what their emotions and thoughts are? Is it possible for the person to measure when their emotions start and stop, and if those feelings lead to thoughts or actions? Is there anything else that needs to be considered other than observing and tracking an individual's emotions and thoughts?

Is there a classifiable way of describing the difference between feelings and emotions, or are they both just things you can feel? Also, does anything else need to be considered?

1.6 A Final Analysis?

So I said in the title that this book would be my 'nal' analysis. What would that mean for the content of the book, however?

In previous articles I discussed how emotions function, how thoughts function and the nature of thoughts, but I did not discuss the nature of feelings. Feelings have a unique nature because each person is different and could describe their feelings completely differently from anyone else. However, my feelings now are much more powerful than they were say a decade ago, before I started on a higher dose of my medications. I just realized what I just said in that last sentence, I don't have the know exactly as to what might give other people stronger emotions, however I did say that being put on harsh or hard medications the last decade made me get stronger and more powerful emotions. Actually I think the medications were supposed to use or suck my energy but I responded by exercising and using them to make myself larger and stronger. I don't know how other people might try to get stronger, medication might be one solution however I don't know how that would work for anyone else, I just know my specific situation. Anyway this is also supposed to be my final analysis, as I said in the title. I've written many other articles on feelings and emotions and thoughts, however that was a long time ago. I think it was just describing the basic functions of feelings and thoughts. The articles went into a lot of detail but most people would probably overlook the basic functions of thoughts and feelings and just head into the experience of feelings and thoughts, so that's why I'm writing this final book, so it would be more practical for people. I've already made my artwork, and the old writing and this nal writing could accompany my artwork, however the artwork more has my own unique detail. This article is written by me, of course, however the artwork is select and more obviously has my detail. So basically, I don't know what else to include as my nal analysis. I've already gone over the difference between emotions, feelings and thoughts however maybe I could go into greater depth about that. There are also certainly other topics that are important in life that I could cover information about. I hope that my artwork gets recognized because these articles don't as obviously have my detail. They could accompany the artwork, however, as both the artwork and articles were done by me.

Is there anything else that I need to cover? I've already pointed out in this article/book the important things about emotions and feelings and thoughts, and how those three relate. That brings up a good point, how much description is enough to describe a persons own emotions and thoughts? Also their thoughts relate and interact with their emotions and feelings. A feeling could cloud an emotion, for instance. That brings up another point, how do emotions and thoughts interact? Furthermore, how much description is necessary in order to address the complications of the interaction between feeling and thought. That relationship has also been described as the relationship between emotion and cognition - which means feeling and thought (that is, emotion means feeling and cognition basically means thought). I've already said that feeling could obscure or cloud thoughts. Thoughts also can lead to feelings, and external actions can also lead to feeling, or cause a person to think about stu and have thoughts. Is it really that simple, however? I mean that is a fairly basic system, thoughts that lead to actions or internal feelings. That is what CBT is anyway, cognitive behavioral therapy is a therapy that works mostly by tracking the persons own internal emotions, and how those emotions lead to thoughts and actions as and then back into emotion, as in a cycle (a cycle of action leading to emotion and emotion leading to thought, or anyone of those leading to the other - either emotion, thought or action can lead to the other in any order in a cycle). So I would think that CBT is a fairly practical therapy then, since it tracks how emotions and thoughts and actions interact. What else would be considered to be practical in life. I mean if someone can track their own internal feelings and thoughts, and how they lead to actions, or how actions lead to internal thoughts and feelings, then I would think that they know most of what they need to know. There are more things going on, however. For instance there are other mental processes like perception, vision and hearing and the relationship between thought and language. Would that describe everything that is going on with someone? Or within someone's own mind? This is basically describing everything that a person can think or everything that is going on in their own mind. Cognitive psychology basically describes the minds mental processes like language, cognition, and perceptions, along with the other mental processes. Cognitive science, however, looks at the mind more from the perspective of how it it is structured. Would that be how the mind functions? It could function from its mental processes of language and perception, and it could function because of its structure or neurology.So that would be figuring out how a mind's neurology is completely configured, that would be the task of neuroscience or a neurologist. That would be fairly important. Other conditions could be treated by a psychologist or a therapist, while a neurologist would look at how the mind is functioning, I would think. That would be a good description of life from the standpoint of how the mind is functioning or how it is working. There is more to life than a person's mind, however.

1.8 Emotions and Feelings

There's a difference between how emotions function and how feelings function in the mind. If an emotion is 'any strong feeling', then any feeling could be described as an emotion. For instance, if someone is in a pool in cold water, then it might be a powerful feeling of water and you could say that the person is experiencing the emotion 'cold'. I would think that feelings are more like sensations however, so the feeling of cold is really just a feeling. I mean how could you compare a sensation to a feeling that is an emotion like happy or sad, fear or anger? So what then is the difference between the sensation of cold and the emotion of feeling 'happy' ? I would think that the feeling of cold is just a sensation. Sensations are more like physical things, like how pain feels or how it feels after a person exercises. What does that make anxiety then? Is anxiety like a sensation? I would think that it could be like the sensation of cold if you feel the anxiety in your body. However, the anxiety might also take the form of a headache. That makes things more complicated - because there are physical sensations and mental sensations, and deeper emotions like happy and sad and anger or surprise or fear that lead to different physiological facial expressions. Those emotions are different from physical sensations because they make you feel things intellectually. Physical sensations can also be intellectual, however. For instance my anxiety can manifest itself in my head and give me a headache, or it could just be a mental anxiety that I feel in my head without any physical pain in my head. There is also pain in the body, which is similar to feelings while during exercise, those physical feelings of exercise could also be painful because they are physical and you can really feel the pain in your body. So what then is the difference between emotions and feelings? Pain is certainly a feeling, and sensations like the sensation of 'cold' is also a feeling in your body. The question is then what makes emotions deep and meaningful, like the emotion of 'happy'. I would think that the emotions 'happy' and 'sad' are simply more intellectual. That is what I said before, that some feelings have intellectual components, I mean even the physical sensation of 'pain' could be intellectual, though I would think that wouldn't be as direct as the feeling of anxiety or the other intellectual emotions of love, happy, sad, fear or anger.

So what is the difference between emotions and feelings then? Is it just the intellectual component? Emotions could have an intellectual component, while some sensations are stupid and don't feel intellectual or 'deep' at all. Those could be described as just feelings like the feeling of 'cold' while emotions could make someone happy like that emotion itself - the emotion 'happy'. What then is the difference between the emotion happy and the emotion sad? Does the emotion sad have components of pain involved? That would be an emotion that is intellectual combined with some physical sensations of pain. The pain in that instance might not be completely physical, however. This is getting a little bit confusing.

There is physical pain, physical sensations, intellectual feelings, and even intellectual sensations like if you have anxiety it could be focused in the head and be like the sensation of pain. Is pain a sensation then, or is it an emotion? Pain is a physical emotion or feeling, and anxiety could be a mental sensation or feeling. SO what are all the different ways of feeling then? There are physical feelings, mental feelings, and there is also sensations and thoughts. A sensation is kind of the opposite of a thought because thoughts are intellectual while sensations are stupid. That is the difference between how sensations feel and how thoughts feel, anyway. There's more to the puzzle, however. Just describing how anxiety feels, how pain feels, and how other emotions like happy or sad feel, and how other feelings or sensations feel like the sensation of 'cold' feel is a good way to start figuring out how all a person's feelings are functioning and making the person feel.

A Further Analysis of Life, Emotions and Everything else! - By Mark Rozen Pettinelli

In my previous article I discussed emotions and feelings, and the difference between a feeling and a thought. I pointed out that emotions can be different from feelings, because emotions are basic and primary, while a feeling is anything that you can feel. So emotions are different from feelings, and sensations are defined as a feeling that comes from something physical. That means that anything physical is a sensation, or a physical sensation. How is that different from any other feeling, however? I mean if there is a physical feeling that a person can get by touching something, then that is a sensation. An emotion, however, might have or cause facial expressions, like how when someone is happy they smile and when someone is sad they frown. Happy and sad are two of the basic primary emotions. Theorists actually disagree over which emotions are the primary ones, however. Though I would say that fear and anger, happy and sad, and surprise are key primary emotions. I mean happy, sad, fear, anger and surprise are some of the most important primary emotions, that is why they are key primary emotions, after all. However, there are many emotions and feelings people can experience, it is subjective to decide which ones are more important than other feelings or emotions, because each person is different from any other person, and might experience any emotion as being different from another person. For instance one person might experience completely different primary emotions from another person if they have a different personality, for instance. For example I respond differently for the emotions of love and caring, maybe those are primary emotions for me while other people might respond with happy or sad or fear. It probably varies based on the person, basically.

So what does that mean the other emotions people experience are like? The primary emotions of happy, sad, fear and surprise could be reactions once they meet another person, or they could be feelings that are felt during a conversation, or at any time in response to any action or activity they are doing. For instance, if they are doing something physical than they might feel pain if they exercise too hard or get tired. So how would sensations t into all of these emotions? I said that sensations are feelings that come from any physical action or touch, like for instance if you touch something you will get a physical sensation. I think what i am trying to do here is describe all the feelings that someone can experience and see how they function with that person. That must have been the influence of my therapists, I've been meeting with professional therapists for years now and I know they have a practical understanding of how the world works because they have to deal with patients or clients that have emotional problems.

2.1 Everything Else?

So what else would I have to talk about here? I've mentioned how feelings are important for people, and how there is a wide variety of sensations, feelings, emotions and thoughts that a person can experience. Furthermore, There is everything in life that the person could be doing - any activity, action or exercise or whatever the person is doing could lead to different sensations or feelings. If it is something physical then it would be called or defined as a 'sensation' because that is how sensations are defined - as a feeling that comes from something physical. So how does all of someone feelings t into their life? There could be a wide variety of feelings that someone could be experiencing at any one time. For instance someone could feel multiple emotions at one time, or at any given moment. So what was I trying to accomplish in this chapter, then? Was I trying to describe all of the feelings that someone could experience and how that ts into the world of life? If there are tons of activities and actions and exercises someone can do - then the question is how do all those feelings that people can experience t into their lives? Exercise can be physical feelings, like if you run hard or sweat or do hard physical work, you could feel physical sensations and other physical feelings. The question is,how do those physical feelings differ from psychological or mental feelings and emotions?

Is a thought different from a physical feeling? Thoughts can be or feel intellectual, while emotions might take longer to experience than any individual or single thought.

The question then is what else needs to be described about life? I mean there is internal activity in the brain like what someone is feeling, and there are external actions and activities and events that occur in th world that might cause the person to experience feelings and thoughts and brain activity.

So I mean, what was I trying to do or describe in this chapter? I think I was trying to gure out all emotions someone could experience, and how those emotions t into the world. There is the external world of objects and actions, and the internal world that is within peoples own minds. The question is, can everything be gured out? Can the external world be figured out, or can the internal world of people's minds be gured out also?

2.2 Anything else?

If there are external actions and objects in the world, and internal worlds of people's minds, then the question is, can everything be figured out? How do emotions occur in people, for instance? If there are a few primary emotions, then the question is, what is important about those emotions? Are those emotions how people respond to things? And do they experience anything else after they feel those emotions? So let's take the primary emotions of happy, sad, anger and fear. Surprise is also one of the primary emotions. How do emotions function, then? What happens rst and then what happens next? I don't really know the answer to that, I would have to think about it. So what happens in an experience? Are there emotions that someone feels in the experience that occur in a certain order or something? There are secondary emotions, which are defined as emotions that occur as a reaction to initial, primary emotions. Does that mean that one of the first emotions people experience are always going to be one of the primary emotions?

So that means that first I am going to feel happy or sad, or angry or surprised, and then i might feel other feelings? How does that work? So what am I trying to figure out here, how emotions occur in people? I would have to know what that person is doing, and what they are like in order to analyze how they feel. I don't even know how I feel about certain emotions or certain activities. The question is, how do people feel about things?

I don't know how I feel about certain activities or actions, for instance. So I guess I'm trying to figure out what the important things in life are, here. I mean I know how I respond to most events, however I don't know what all of my emotions are like. This is starting to sound a little bit selfish. I mean, most people have to work hard in life, it

isn't like life is all fun and games.

Chapter 3
Mark Xiornik Rozen Pettinelli Reviews Cognitive Psychology Research Articles

What is science or communication? Science is important because it is basically a rigorous or thorough understanding. What could someone achieve a thorough understanding of ? If you think about it, if something needs to be communicated then you need to first understand it. First something is thought about, then it is thought about more deeply, and then it is understood. That makes sense. If you think about it - when someone thinks about something for the first time a type of understanding dawns on them. This understanding takes a certain period of time to figure out, however. How long does it take for someone to figure something out? That is an interesting question, in order to figure out something someone might need to make sentences in their head or think about something with words. They might also make or think about sounds to themself - think the sentence out in their head with sounds, for instance. That process could enhance how the understanding of a certain concept is thought about or understood (figured out).

That is a good question, how exactly is something 'figured out' ? It is probably more complicated than just saying the sentence of it to themselves in their heads.

For instance if someone thinks about something with words then that can help them to understand something. However it isn't as if someone just says to themself, 'well if I think about it this way or that way, or if I think about this or that thing then I could understand this concept or idea better'.

Sometimes people need help understanding concepts or ideas from other people or influences in their environment. What kind of influence does other people have on humans' understanding of concepts? Understanding concepts is important, what kind of idea is someone trying to understand? That is a good question, if you think about it logically then all the ideas in life can be sorted through and organized, and it could be figured out how difficult it is to understand each different idea.

How then would someone sort through all of the ideas in life and organize or categorize them? They could do it in various ways, I would think that they could it based upon which ideas are hard to understand, and also which ideas have similar physical objects - for instance you could label something physical an idea - say the idea of a 'house' A house is a physical object. Then would every word that there is in the English language, or in any language for that matter, be an idea? Every word in the language is an idea, and each word or idea also has a definition.That is, just like every word there is has a definition, every idea also has a definition. Take the word 'I', the word "I" refers to the person who is saying the word, it means themself, "I" basically just means "me". That is an example of a word that has a definition.

The definition of the word "I" is a person who is referring to themself. It is an idea, it is the concept of yourself or it is simply you referring to yourself. Objects can be ideas Similarly, any object can be an idea. Take the object of a house. "Houses" can be ideas just like they are objects. The idea of a house could be a place to live where you are happy, and the definition of a house could be a place to live where you can be happy, or sad, or any type of condition. The idea of a house is more selective, it is the idea of the house that is occurring to you at that time, while the definition of the house is similar, the definition of a house is place you can live with a certain type of condition or a certain type of house with various objects, while a different idea of a house could occur to different people. So basically different people could have different ideas of houses for themselves, while there would only be one good definition of a house that is descriptive. That means that objects can be ideas. An object is anything in life that has a physical presence, and since you can think about anything in life that is physical, then it can be an idea in your head. The idea you have in your head could be different from the object however. That is why certain objects are described as 'phallic' symbols, those objects basically represent penises. They are shaped elongated in real life, so in the persons mind they change them into the shape of a phallus (basically a penis).

That is probably the best example of how objects in real life have definitions, and they also can change when a person thinks about them, because they be-come ideas in the persons head. Objects and ideas are important for dentions

This means that objects and ideas are important for a persons understand of a words definition. Also, not only do words have definitions, but since objects can be words, then objects also have definitions. I already said that an object in real life can be altered in a persons mind - how they think about that object is po-tentially different from what the object is like in real life, for instance. If you think about it scientifically or objectively, every-thing in the world can be an individual object, and every individ-ual object can be thought about in a persons mind. However, how the person thinks about objects often differs from what the ob-ject actually does in the real world.

Concepts are important for Comprehension

Understanding concepts is important for comprehension. For instance its important to understand ideas and concepts if some-one wants to understand, well, what the idea is.

But what is it that someone is trying to understand?

Is it the idea or is it the physical object or phenomena? There could be something physical that is present in real life that the person is trying to understand, say a house or the construction of a house could be a complicated thing that someone is trying to understand. Or, however, someone could be trying to understand what houses mean to them, like safety and a place to live. There are physical properties that could be understood with things or there could be mental concepts and ideas that could be compre-hended with stu. That months' articles discusses memory and how it relates to vision and cognition. If you think about it mem-ory is going to relate to the other cognitive processes like vision and cognition. I mean, there are only so many cognitive processes

- especially major ones. That might be subjective, however, depending upon how you would dene a 'major' cognitive process.

3.1 An Introduction to Ideas

There are many topics in education. Life can be described academically in dierent ways

and can be categorized - for every category that life can be divided into there is also a way to describe that category (the material, stu and ideas that make up that section of 'life').

What would be a simple way of organizing life or categorizing it? Psychology is the study of the mind or the study of life. There are also mental functions, humans perceive and feel their world around them. If you consider those factors - that humans perceive and interpret, and that there is material objects in the world around them, then the logical conclusion is that life primarily and fundamentally consists of humans observing the world.

Mark Pettinelli Northeastern University This assignment was prepared for

course ENG 1105: College Writing I by Professors Barbara Ohrstrom; Justin

Senter; Seth Stair 6/25/17

Working title: Can a categorization of different topics in Cognitive Psychology lead to a better understanding of the mind and categorization itself: can important information be sorted? Broad subject: Organize intellectual academic information in cognitive psychology and general academic categories (especially those related to the study of the mind) Thesis: Epistemology or the study of knowledge could be difficult or complex to study; in order to sort through important information someone would need to organize the different topics and the relevant information that falls under those headings/categories. Buxbaum, Otto. (2016). Key Insights into Basic Mechanisms of Mental Activity. Springer International Publishing AG Switzerland. This book discusses the mind and how it thinks it describes how the mind uses judgements and concepts and memories to think in everyday activities. That is useful for this essay about

figuring out how to sort through important information because the information that needs

to be sorted is cognitive information in the mind. The mind itself sorts through information

and this book talks about basic concepts the mind understands that helps it think like

judgements, concepts and memories.

Mental activity is discussed in the book and how it uses concepts and memory structures. In order to understand how the mind sorts through information it would need to be understood how the minds concepts and memory structures are formed.The book talks about mental activity and cognitive psychology, and while it tries to connect cognition and behavior I think that it is important to connect behavior to how information is sorted since behavior (or action) is how information is gathered. Sprevak, Mark and Kallestrup, Jesper (editors). (2014) New waves in philosophy of Mind. Palgrave Macmillan, England. This book discusses, as is in the title, `philosophy of mind'. Philosophy of mind is important to the study of intelligence and categorization because it includes a discussion of consciousness and intelligence. Intelligence is part of consciousness so thought, intellect and consciousness are discussed at length in the book. Those topics would help to advance the point of this essay which is to explain how minds categorize information. In order to understand how a mind categorizes information it is necessary to understand what it is like for someone to be conscious and to think. What it is like for someone to be conscious is described throughout the book. The book describes the material stu about consciousness called 'phenomenology' and the non-material stu that is more mental and related to the concepts people use and what they think about.

Kevin Mccain. (2016). The Nature of Scientific Knowledge. Springer International Publishing AG Switzerland.

This book discusses, like the title of the book says, the 'nature' of scientific knowledge. It is important to understand what is scientific in learning material and any sort of understanding because it helps to make it more clear and, well, scientific. That relates to the point of this essay which is to clarify knowledge and figure out how the mind sorts through different types of information. If knowledge is scientific then does the mind figure out knowledge and information in a scientific fashion? The book talks about different ways to understand and figure out what makes certain types of information 'scientific'. What makes information clear and understood that is a question that the book addresses. If information is understood then I wonder how the mind would 'understand' the information. Information is thought about in the mind differently from how it is discussed in public, for example.

Carver, Charles and Cheier, Michael. (2013) Attention and Self-Regulation: A Control-Theory Approach to Human Behavior. Springer International Publishing AG Switzerland. The title of the book is 'attention and self-regulation' and it should be mentioned that by definition self-regulation is how the mind regulates itself, and when you combine attention with self-regulation then it is an implied understanding that it is how the mind works when it pays attention and thinks about regulating itself. The book is basically about the processes the mind uses when it focuses on itself, when it sorts through information that is within the persons own mind, for instance the book says it is about the 'self ', and how the information in the mind gets sorted through. That obviously relates to the point of this essay because if someone is going to gure out how the mind sorts through information it needs to think about how it the mind pays attention and regulates itself.

Mark Pettinelli Problem/Solution Essay Northeastern University Author Note This essay was prepared for course ENG 1105: College Writing I by Professors Barbara Ohrstrom; Justin Senter; Seth Stair The problem I've had since I graduated high school was basically boredom. I got anxious, high anxiety because I had nothing to do and tried to solve it by doing cognitive psychology and philosophy of mind research. I thought to myself that all the information in academics and life could be sorted and more easily understood, and in this way I could x my mind and make myself think more clearly and be much less anxious. I think that some of my problem had to do with what Tversky and Kahneman called approximation and adjustment (quoted from (Carver and Cheier (2013)): A second judgment heuristic discussed by Tversky and Kahneman (1974) may be called approximation and adjustment. This is the process of beginning an estimate by making a first approximation, and then reaching a nal judgment by adjusting this approximation some-what. The first approximation may be based on a partial computation (or partial decision), or it may be suggested by the form of the problem (or the decision being undertaken). I basically kept thinking to myself the same thing over and over and that was part of the problem of figuring out how to think about logic and intelligence. I kept having to think about the same thing over and over, the same topic in academics, however I used `approximation and adjustment' to think about what I was thinking. For instance, I had a topic in mind and thought about it, then thought about it a second time a little differently, and kept repeating this process throughout the day or week.

3.2 Problem of Boredom

So I basically solved my problem of boredom for the last decade (2006-2017) by thinking about cognitive psychology and philosophy of mind research. I posted my results here on connexions (you can review my modules here)

3.3 What is the 'understood' part of Comprehension?

Insert paragraph text here.

This is a good question, what about understanding or comprehension is complicated or complex? It could be described neurologically, however most people would not understand the biological details involved. I wouldn't either. I could try to describe it in a simple fashion, or in a fashion that just involves the analog understanding. I will say what i mean by 'analog understanding' in the next paragraph. Information can be understood, that is what could be understood - one could say that there are different types of information. Some information is analog, that is, it is made up of stuff- it doesn't have specific mathematical components, but is more like puddy.

That is a good way that I can describe an understanding, it can be a mathematical understanding or a conceptual understanding. Conceptual understandings involve concepts and different types of information. Understandings that are analog do not necessarily involve any information but could just be descriptive or have stu, have components that are not informative or not complex. Analog by definition means not digital, so an analog understanding would be an understanding that does not necessarily have or not have information, but has stu that can be manipulated nondigitally, like say with your hands.

Analog vs. Digital

I haven't used the terms 'analog' and 'digital' to apply to types of understanding, however they can be applied to types of information. However, since understanding stu is understanding information then the terms analog and digital can be applies to the term 'understand' or 'comprehend'. For instance when someone understands anything it is actually both digital and analog, it is digital because it consists of a set of information, and it is analog because it is made up of stu, stu in the persons mind and the stu that the person is trying to understand.

So analog is anything that is not digital, that is not numerical.

Numerical means that it consists of numbers. Or does that mean that it can be read and described with numbers? It could mean either I suppose. That means that a digital watch is a watch with digits, and an analog clock is a clock with a hand instead of a digital watch with digits. That helps describe the difference between analog and digital.

3.4 What is Comprehension?

Comprehension is anything that is understood or figured out. Basically that means that there is a type of processing that the mind does whereby it understands different types of information (in life). If the mind understands different kinds of information, then what are those categories of

information? O the top of my head I don't know all of them, however there are several

obvious main categories of information in life such as foods, clothes, objects, buildings, streets

and cars, nature, and art.

It depends how you want to describe the different topics in life, basically.

The different topics in life can be described depending on various values or definitions.

Depending on what the person is trying to achieve or describe or dene, in other words. I

just described some categories based o of how I think a person's mind categorizes information

for itself, that is one way to describe the different categories in life.

Categories in Life

Basically you can describe different categories in life. This is a good way to simplify how one thinks about things, if you think about it. In other words in order to think clearly someone might first need to categorize.

What might someone categorize? Furthermore, if someone wants to think with clarity (think clearly) then how would they go about organizing their minds with the proper information?

I have some ideas of my own about how someone could do something like that. It was based on my own thinking and how I have been thinking with my own mind.

Basically there can be different priorities, in other words the mind can think based upon

different categorizations of information or priorities. Those priorities could be emotional and motivational or priorities about how they want to think about information, or what kinds of information they want to think about.

If you think about it, intelligent humans might want to think about information in addition

to wanting to have emotions and ideas that they ponder and accept. Is that cognitive science

and psychology? That is basically describing how the mind thinks and feels.

How does the mind think and feel?

That is a good question, how does the mind think and feel anyway? It depends on what the person is focusing on at any moment. If someone is only focusing on one thing, then that is the thing that they are thinking or feeling at that time.

However it is much more complicated than that I supposed, how would the mind organize itself to think and feel, if it wants to think and feel at any one time then? It isn't as if the mind is a simple organ that simply feels basic feelings and thinks basic thoughts at any given time.

The mind is complicated and it processes information and feelings in a complicated fashion. I would say that is accurate based o of the information of the minds many different functions, feelings and ideas.

Some of those ideas are motivations about the people around them or their environment, and some of the information that they think about could also be about their environment, or it could come from memories or previously learned ideas and thoughts.

Ideas and Thoughts can be Figured out

Different ideas and thoughts that occur to people can be figured out, basically. Sometimes those ideas or thoughts could be previously learned or simply take more time to figure out than instant ideas and thoughts that occur to them momentarily.

So I just mentioned that an idea or a thought could take different amounts of time to figure out. That means that it also is learned at some point. If an idea that someone has is an idea that takes them time to learn then it could be an old idea that learned a long (or brief) time ago. I would say there is a difference between previously learned ideas and previously learned emotions and feelings and new ideas, thoughts and feelings.

Humans think with concepts

Basically that means that people think with concepts. something that a person learns or thinks about? What is a concept then? Is it If you think about it, at any one time someone is thinking about information or processing feelings (or some combination of the two).

If you think about how many feelings a person has, and how many ideas they can think about, then they could be feeling a complicated set of feelings and thinking about (or processing) a lot of information at any one time.

What kind of description is that? I just said that humans have tons of feelings and can think

about lots of stuff. Does that mean that they have a large capacity of feeling and thought or something?

How then does the mind process those feelings and thoughts? If you think about, its about input and output, and a central processor. The central processor is the mind, the input in the environment, and the output is their behavior and thoughts.

Chapter 4
Emotions and Feelings and How to
Change Them

Emotion is more similar to conscious thought than feelings are to conscious thought. Although emotion and feeling can be described as unconscious thought, one of them is going to be more similar to conscious thought. Feelings are more like sensations, when you touch something you get a feeling. Therefore feelings are faster than emotions and thought, because when you touch something there is a slight delay before you can think of something about it (thought), or feel something deeply about it (emotion). Emotion is therefore just unconscious thought.

Actually it would better be described as unconscious feeling (so a feeling is like a conscious emotion because you can "feel" it better and easier but emotion is a deeper, more unconscious experience similar to unconscious thought, but emotions are also more similar to conscious thought because thought is a deep experience while feelings are intense or shallow, but not deep).

One definition of emotion can be "any strong feeling". From that description many conclusions can be drawn. Basic (or primary) emotions can be made up of secondary emotions like love can contain feelings or emotions of lust, love and longing. Feelings can be described in more detail than emotions because you can have a specific feeling for anything, each feeling is unique and might not have a name.

For instance, if you are upset by one person that might have its own feeling because that person upsets you in a certain way. That feeling doesn't have a defined name because it is your personal feeling. The feeling may also be an emotion, say anger. "Upset" is probably too weak to be an emotion, but that doesn't mean that it isn't strong like emotions are strong in certain ways. Cold is also just a feeling. There is a large overlap between how feelings feel and how emotions feel, they are similar in nature. So there are only a few defined emotions, but there are an infinite number ways of feeling things. You can have a "small" emotion of hate and you could say that you have the feeling hate then, if it is large you could say you are being emotional about hate, or are experiencing the emotion hate. You can have the same emotion of hate in different situations, but each time the feeling is going to be at least slightly different.

You can recognize any feeling, that is what makes it a feeling. If you are sad that is a feeling, but if you are depressed that isn't a feeling it is more like an emotion. You can't identify why you are depressed but you can usually identify why you are sad. Feelings are more immediate, if something happens or is happening, it is going to result in a feeling. However, if something happened a long time ago, you are going to think about it unconsciously and that is going to bring up unconscious feelings. Otherwise known as emotion. So emotions are unconscious feelings that are the result of unconscious thoughts. Feeling defined there as something you can identify. So you can't identify the unconscious thought that caused the unconscious feeling, but you can identify the unconscious feeling (aka emotion).

Another aspect of unconscious thought, emotion, or unconscious feeling (all three are the same) is that it tends to be mixed into the rest of your system because it is unconscious. If it was conscious then it remains as an individual feeling, but in its unconscious form you confuse it with the other emotions and feelings and it affects your entire system. So therefore most of what people are feeling is just a mix of feelings that your mind cannot separate out

individually. That is the difference between sadness and a depression, a depression lowers your mood and affects all your feelings and emotions, but sadness is just that individual feeling. So the reason that the depression aects all your other feelings is because you can no longer recognize the individual sad emotions that caused it. The feelings become mixed.

If someone can identify the reason they are sad then they become no longer depressed, just sad. Once they forget that that was the reason they are depressed however, they will become depressed again.

That is why an initial event might make someone sad, and then that sadness would later lead into a depression, is because you forget why you originally got sad. You might not consciously forget, but unconsciously you do. That is, it feels like you forget, the desire to get revenge on whatever caused the sadness fades away. When that happens it is like you forgetting what caused it. You may also consciously forget but what matters is how much you care about that sadness. It might be that consciously understanding why you are depressed or sad changes how much you care about your sadness, however. That would therefore change the emotion/feeling of sadness. The more you care about the sadness/depression, the more like a feeling it becomes and less like an emotion. That is because the difference between feelings and emotions is that feelings are easier to identify (because you can feel them easier).

The following is a good example of the transition from caring about a feeling to not caring about a feeling. Anger as an emotion takes more energy to maintain, so if someone is punched or something, they are only likely to be mad for a brief period of time, but the sadness that it incurred might last for a much longer time. That sadness is only going to be recognizable to the person punched for a brief period of time as attributable to the person who did the punching, after that the sadness would sink into their system like a miniature depression.

Affecting the other parts of their system like a depression.

In review, both feelings and emotions are composed of unconscious thoughts, but feelings are easier to identify than emotions. Feelings are faster than emotions in terms of response (the response time of the feeling, how fast it responds to real world stimulation) and it takes someone less time to recognize feelings because they are faster. Feelings are closer to sensory stimulation, if you touch something, you feel it and that is a fast reaction. You care about the feeling so you can separate it out in your head from the other feelings. You care in that sentence could be translated into, the feeling is intense, so you feel it and can identify it easily.

That is different from consciously understanding why you are depressed or sad.

You can consciously understand why you are depressed or sad, but that might or might not affect the intensity of that sadness.If the intensity of the sadness is brought up enough, then you can feel that sadness and it isn't like a depression anymore, it is more like an individual feeling then something that affects your mood and brings your system down (aka a depression).

Also, if you clearly enough understand what the sadness is then it is going to remain a sadness and not affect the rest of your system. That is because the feeling would get mixed in with the other feelings and start affecting them. The period of this more clear understanding of the sadness mostly occurs right after the event that caused the sadness. That is because it is clear to you what it is. Afterwards the sadness might emerge (or translate from a depression, to sadness) occasionally if you think about what caused it or just think about it in general. The difference between emotion and feeling is that feelings are easier to identify because they are faster, a feeling is something you are feeling right then. An emotion might be a deeper experience because it might affect more of you, but that is only because it is mixed into the rest of your system. That is, a depression affects more of you than just an isolated feeling of sadness. In other words, people can only have a few feelings at a time, but they can have many emotions at the same time. Emotions are mixed in, but to feel something you have to be able to identify what it is, or it is going to be so intense that you would be able to identify what it is. Emotions just feel deeper because it is all your feelings being affected at once.

Since emotion is all your feelings being affected at once, emotions are stronger than feelings. Feelings however are a more directed focus. When you feel something you can always identify what that one thing is. When you have an emotion, the emotion is more distant, but stronger. All your feelings must feel a certain way about whatever is causing the emotion. So that one thing is affecting your entire system. Feelings can then be defined as immediate unconscious thought, and emotions as unconscious thought.

•

When you care about an emotion, you could say that you have a higher attention for

emotion or that emotional event during that time. You are probably going to be in a

higher state of action readiness, that is, you are probably more alert and going to be

able to respond faster to whatever it is you are focusing on, or just respond faster in

general. You also are going to have a better understanding of the emotion if you care

about it more - you make an assessment of the emotions strength and its nature when you think about the emotion (or the event that generated the emotion).

Feelings are more direct than emotions and thought because they are more sensory when you touch something you get a feeling.

That shows further how emotions are really about things in the real world, only it more like you are thinking about them instead of feeling them in real time.

Things that come from memory are going to be emotions and/or thoughts, not feelings because feelings are things which are more tangible, those memories might result in new feelings, but the memories themselves are not feelings because they are just thoughts.

That shows how you can feel some things more than others, that thought and feeling are indeed separate and intelligence is sometimes driven by feelings and emotions, and sometimes it isn't. You can think about things and not have feelings guiding those thoughts Or your feelings could be assisting your thoughts.

If you care about a feeling then it becomes easier to identify it that shows how your feelings can help you to identify other feelings, so your emotions contribute to your emotional intelligence.

If a certain emotion is larger than others then to your intellect it is going to be easier to recognize, and easier to think about (that is why a depression feels like it does, because you don't know the individual emotions contributing to it so you cannot feel a specific emotion of sadness from it.

An explanation for this chapter:
So feelings are easier to "feel" than emotions, that is probably why they are called feelings, because you "feel" them better. Maybe someone else thinks you can feel emotions easier, I don't know, the point is you can feel emotions and feelings with different levels of intensity and in more than one way, a feeling could be not intense but clear to you. So how conscious you are of the feeling or emotion influences the intensity of it and your conscious experience of it. A feeling could be more intense than en emotion if it is the only thing you are feeling as well. That makes sense, if an emotion is very complicated, then you probably couldn't feel the entire thing as clearly in a brief period of time. So my theory is that feelings are more simple, and therefore there are more shallow but possibly more intense than emotion because you can focus on a simple thing easier.

If you are having a deep emotional experience (experiencing an emotion) then it makes sense that you aren't as in touch with all of those feelings that are occurring. When you touch something you get the feeling "cold" - that is simple to understand.When you are in a depression you don't understand all the complicated emotions that you are experiencing. You could experience sadness all day. When you can say "oh, I really "felt" that", then you know you feel it and it is a feeling.

When you feel something, it is a feeling.

When you are emotional about something, those are feelings too, but it is more powerful and deeper, you aren't as in touch will all of it because it is more complex. You could be in touch with something complex and feel that too, I guess. Though I would argue that a feeling is easier to focus on if it is simple and clear to understand and feel to your conscious mind.

The significance of this chapter:

If someone is emotional, then they are feeling a lot. I could say that the emotions someone is experiencing could be brought up at different times and felt more - translated from somewhere in your strong emotions to something you feel more closely. So you can feel some things but that doesn't mean that the feeling is intense or clear - those things might become clear however at some point. When those emotions become clear and you 'bring them up' - either by caring about the emotion or the thought that represents it or it just emerges by some other method (such as by doing an evaluation of your emotional state) - then they become feelings because you can feel them easier. These feelings are more clear, similar to when you touch something you get a feeling that is simple and tactile. That is why feelings are called the result of emotions, because emotions are like the basis for feelings (at least non-tactile ones). You might have a feeling that has a shallow source however as well I would say. It doesn't have to be that a feeling is first felt deeply, and then you feel it more clearly later on (the feeling being the result of an emotion). Maybe the feeling is simple at first and then it becomes more complex later.

What role does attention have to play? Being emotional or feeling something can make you pay more or less attention to things, including other feelings. Your attention can naturally rise just because of your emotional state.

People feel emotions, and they can feel feelings. Emotions are strong and the powerful source of human behavior, and while feelings are also powerful they are also diverse, curious, and unique - 'old feelings returning'.

4.1 How to Change Emotions and Feelings

An appraisal is when you assess something. People make appraisals or assessments of emotion
all of the time, however they aren't aware most of the time that they are doing this. How much someone cares about an emotional stimulus is something that is probably thought about frequently during the experience. If you think about it people frequently are going to naturally analyze what is going on in every situation they are in and think about what the emotions occurring are.

I said in the previous paragraph that people make appraisals of emotional things but they aren't aware of themselves doing that. How is that possible or what does that mean exactly?

If people care about emotion, which they clearly do, then they are going to want to know what is going on in the situations they encounter in life. So clearly people make assessments of how much emotion the things around them are generating, the only question is can they do this in a way that is beneath their awareness.

People surely must make assessments since they often work on inducing or inhibiting feelings in order to make them "appropriate" to a situation. If you are going to be changing feeling, then obviously you are going to need to measure and assess it first. Sometimes people think this process through consciously, and sometimes they don't.

It makes sense to me that people are going to "know" how valuable certain things in their environment are. This is clear when you realize that people focus on some things very quickly - such a thing would clearly be something of interest to that person or something that generates emotion - which would make it interesting.

So you could say that a person whose attention gets alerted to something around them made an assessment about the stimulus or responded to it, the stimulus (the thing in their environment they paid sharp attention to) was clearly emotional for them.

It could have generated any feeling - disgust, surprise, happiness, - or maybe an intellectual reaction such as 'that person has a bright coat'. Does that mean that the person assessed if the bright coat generated emotion for them? What would it mean if it generated emotion? Could they respond in a fast way without being interested? Someone could respond quickly to something and not be in a mood that is very caring at that time, in which case maybe little emotion was involved.

However if someone was interested in something then it makes sense that it is going to cause them to have feelings. Is something someone is interested in going to cause them to have deep emotions or shallow feelings? What types of stimuli result in deep or shallow feelings? Just because something generates more emotion for you doesn't necessarily mean that it is going to cause you to

respond to it faster or you would be more interested in it.

Maybe your interest is more intellectual or maybe you are interested or responding to it quickly because you have to.

Under what circumstances do people care more about feelings? This relates to appraisals

- if you care about something then you are going to make more assessments during the

experience about how much emotion is being generated probably.

People can care more about feelings but that doesn't mean that they are aware that they care more during that time. This is similar to people going into modes where they are seeking pleasure. My theory here is that people have levels of desire and need that fluctuate constantly.

This means that there are many different levels someone can experience an emotion or feeling.

It is more complicated than simply saying that the feeling has a certain strength - each feeling

or emotion is going to have a unique nature, represent unique ideas and objects, and have a unique significance on your psyche.

Maybe you can say that there are shallow feelings and deep emotions, and that there are certain properties that shallow feelings have and certain properties that deep feelings have. For instance you probably care more about deep feelings (unless the feeling is negative) and therefore they probably cause you to have a faster reaction time. However if the feeling is deep, sappy, and emotional then maybe your reaction time is slower because the emotion is weighing you down.

This relates to the 'emotions and feelings and the difference between them' section above because I am outlining further that deep feelings/emotions or shallow feelings/emotions are different and things happen to humans differently with each one.

It shows that clearly emotion can make someone be different physically, as when you are motivated by emotion you often move faster.

This is just bringing up ideas of depth - some feelings are simple and some are complex - that is obvious, however I think people could notice a lot more if they grouped their emotions into a categories of strength and shallowness or depth and how they responded differently to each different category. - Also the person should note what the interest was, the reaction time, the negative or positive valence of the emotion.

Goffman suggests that we spend a good deal of effort on managing impressions - that is, acting. Your impression of other people makes you feel in different ways, and you try to manage this in a social situation. So therefore all of your strong feelings you try to influence by thinking about what caused those feelings - such as your impressions - and how you can change them.

So people are basically "emotion-managers", constantly thinking about their feelings and what caused them and how they can change them. Whenever you change an impression of someone, you are also changing your feelings. When you think about your own feelings you are changing them because you are changing how much you care about them. You set goals for yourself about your own feelings - 'if I do this I am going to become happy'.

When you think about your feelings you can make insignificant feelings large or large feelings small. When a feeling is small, you could say that it is more unconscious or beneath your awareness. Something (including yourself) could trigger this small feeling and it could emerge into something you feel more closely and more consciously.

So the question is, what circumstances and what type of thinking warrant that feeling of 'that sort'. We assess the 'appropriateness' of a feeling by making a comparison between the feeling and the situation. We also have goals for how we want to feel that we don't know we are thinking, and we have goals for how we want to act as well. Is there a 'natural attitude' or a natural way of behaving and thinking? Not really - especially when you consider that you are unconsciously constantly creating goals, drives, thoughts and behaviors that are not fully under your control.

In secondary reactive emotions, the person reacts against his or her initial primary adaptive emotion, so that it is replaced with a secondary emotion. This "reaction to the reaction" obscures or transforms the original emotion and leads to actions that are not entirely appropriate to the current situation. For example, a man that encounters danger and begins to feel fear may feel that fear is not "manly." He may then either become angry at the danger (externally focused reaction) or angry with himself for being afraid (self-focused reaction), even when the angry behavior actually increases the danger. Listening to this reaction, someone is likely to have the sense that "something else is going on here" or "there's more to this than just anger." The experience is something like hearing two different melodies being played at the same time in a piece of music, one the main melody and the other the background or counterpart.

-
-

Secondary emotions often arise from attempts to judge and control primary responses. Thus, anxiety may come from trying to avoid feeling angry or sexually excited, or it may arise from guilt about having felt these emotions.

When someone rejects what they are truly feeling, they are likely to feel bad about themselves. Feeling or expressing one emotion to mask the primary emotion is a meta emotional process. Feelings about emotions need to be acknowledged and then explored to get at the underlying primary emotion.

Experiential therapists see clients emotional processing as occurring on a continuum with five phases (Kennedy-Moore + Watson, 1999):

1. prereective reaction to an emotion-eliciting stimulus entailing perception of the stimulus, preconscious cognitive and emotional processing, and accompanying physiological
changes
2. conscious awareness and perception of the reaction
3. labeling and interpretation of the aective response; people typically draw upon internal as well as situational cues to label their responses
4. evaluation of whether the response is acceptable or not
5. evaluation of the current context in terms of whether it is possible or desirable to reveal
one's feelings.

What role does the emotion 'interest' play in emotional responses? It is a baseline emotion of great importance - the action tendency of interest involves intending, orienting, and exploring. Interest is felt very frequently, probably without being noticed. If you think about it, to some degree interest is going to be present with each reaction to stimuli. With every response someone has, they are interested to some degree. You can look at interest further when you consider secondary emotional responses - what was the interest that came from the response that had some other type of interest?

Through each stage of evaluation of a response, or simple evaluations that aren't a response to things, there is interest involved as well. This 'interest' induces caring, and the interest and caring is going to change your emotions - emotions are going to be brought up, intensified, changed based on your interest or caring or evaluations.

2 Kennedy-Moore, E., + Watson, J.C. (1999).
New York: Guilford Press.

Expressing emotion:

When you think and make evaluations, you change the nature and intensity of the emotions that are related to what you are doing or processing.

Are people going to be more interested in clear, primary emotions or feelings that they aren't in touch with?

When someone is interested in a feeling, how is that different from being interested in the source of the feeling? If someone is feeling sad, they might not care about the sadness if the feeling is unclear to them or they don't know they are sad. If someone is going to try to change a feeling of sadness, it clearly would be beneficial if they knew when the feeling is occurring.

Is it possible to experience deep emotions without being aware at all that these emotions

are occurring? Yes it is, but there are times when people are conscious of those emotions say when they are recalling them - that the deep emotions are more clear. There could be a

deep emotion that occurs over a long period of time - say anger at someone, this anger could

be in your body for a long time, during being the person, or while away from the person;

the point is the anger is reflected upon or it occurs more deeply at certain points - and then you are going to be aware of the emotion.

That anger is a significant, primary feeling. The feeling is significant because it shows how

large the emotion is that is behind it. People can feel feelings that are shallow or intense

at the time, but these feelings don't necessarily mean more than that or are deeper than

that because they aren't deep or primary - they don't mean anything else or occur at other times you aren't aware of (indicating that this feeling is significant). The feeling of shallow feelings is still potent (because you are feeling them in real time), but they aren't as powerful as feelings that have a special meaning or significance for you (which would make you feel deeper in real time and feel more effected).

If you think about it, people change their feelings by thinking all of the time. The way they could help manage this is probably by making assessments of their emotional state. If people think about what just made them happy or sad, then they might be able to do something or think something to change that. Some emotional responses are going to be more noticeable, and that is when people might try to figure out what went on.

There are subtleties of emotion as well. People probably respond in many ways that they aren't aware of consciously, but they might have responded because something beneath their notice occurred emotionally. You could say that the emotional world beneath your notice is the "unconscious" mind or the unconscious world.

Your emotions change all of the time, only sometimes are you going to notice when an emotion changes or when you are experiencing one.

Furthermore, you might want or expect to experience one emotion but you are actually experiencing a different one because unconsciously that is how you are responding. For instance, maybe you have an unconscious bias against a group of people so you feel hate when you interact with them, but you consciously think that you like those people and feel like you should be happy and positive towards them.

A feeling might be important to your unconscious mind, or a feeling might be important to your conscious mind - in which case you would probably 'care' about it.

Your attention is constantly divided between various things in your environment, your own internal thinking and your own emotions. Your emotions are going to determine and assist what you pay attention to. For instance, if something is emotional in your environment for you, then more of your attention is probably going to spent thinking about or focusing on that thing.

Or maybe something in your environment is just more interesting than something else, the point is something in your environment or something in your head (emotions, thoughts) caused an intellectual or emotional reaction in you, and that then caused you to pay more attention to it. That doesn't mean that you notice it more after you pay attention - this type of paying attention might be unconscious - i.e. - more of your attentional resources or just more of the focus that people have (not all of which they are aware of) is going to be directed at it.

References
Emotion-Focused Therapy: Coaching Clients to Work Through Their Feelings. Leslie Greenberg. Amer Psychological Assn; 1 edition (January 2002)

Some Notes
By
Mark Pettinelli

So I am trying to think. How exactly does the mind work? I think I need to understand how the mind functions in order to think clearly. There is cognition, which is how people think, and there are emotions, which determine how people feel.

But is that all I need to know about the mind in order to function? The mind must be more complicated than just the experience of feelings and thoughts.

So I did a lot of research, they're books in my room about cognitive psychology and cognitive science and related topics in psychology. Like cognition and emotion, concepts etc.

Is that all I need to know? Is there any more research I can do? Do I need to know anything else? That's an excellent question.

I did a lot of research. I read books on cognitive science and cognitive psychology. I did a ton of research, what did I figure out again. There were books on cognitive psychology, and books on emotion and cognition. THere were also books about logic and clear thinking, or critical thinking. There was one book on concepts that I liked.

So I don't know what exactly I learned or figured out, how the mind works maybe? I mean now I understand logic and emotions or psychology and clear thinking. What else do I need to learn in order to progress myself. I did the research by myself, only now am I being guided. But those articles written by me were written before I started to be guided. I mean they just figured out the rest of the academics, some of it was academics I was trying to teach. I think their logic was sort of like, well we have all the information, having fun is more important than information anyway so we can try to have now and increase that and change that, so it doesn't really matter if the stupid information is over. That seems to be what they're thinking, that's also what I am thinking right now.

On the other hand, maybe the information could also continue. Concepts are complicated, I can continue to develop the intellectual aspect. The question is, do I need to become more intelligent? Maybe I could just develop the physical aspect, I don't know.

So do I need to become more intelligent. How have I become intelligent so far, I've become more conscious of myself and my mind. I am aware of what I am thinking and what I am feeling. I mean as a kid I didn't even know what the definition of 'emotion regulation' was, I did have emotions, but wasn't aware that I was having those emotions. Now I am aware of my emotions and my thoughts and try to change them, understand them and experience them.

That's mostly how I've become more intelligent over the years. I don't know if I could be even more aware of my emotions and thoughts, or if that's necessary. How else could I become more intelligent then?

Um so maybe the research is over, I mean i've already said that they seem to think having fun is more important, and that can increase and improve over the future years. It doesn't matter that the new information is over, that's what I'm used to, I was providing all (or most of) the new info. Now I think it's more fun to just increase the amount of fun and change that up.

Now that all the academics have finished my life has improved, they use to keep asking me to make money. What a bunch of dumbasses. Now the academics are over. They think they can copy me by putting other people in a lot of pain, but they forgot that I was born at the beginning of time so my birth was unique. They won't be able to get anyone else from the beginning of time because I was the only one who survived.

I don't know if i need to become more intelligent, i've already mastered most of the stuff i need to know.

Once again, I've already become intelligent, I don't know if I need to learn anything else.

Um so once again they think they can copy me by torturing someone else, however my birth was completely different, so was most of the experience that happened in ancient history. It was a lot of pain and anxiety.

I'm trying to think, I think because my birth was different they won't be able to copy me. Tons of people go through lots of pain however my birth and most of the experience was done at the beginning of time, or a really long time ago, I think that seems to be the case.

Um so that means they have to keep me alive. I'm the only one from the beginning of time.

I don't know if i need to become more intelligent. I don't know if I need to do anymore research. I've already become more conscious and am aware of my emotions. I told you before when I was a child I didn't even know what the word 'emotion regulation' meant. Now I have a really good understanding of emotion regulation and what it means.

Um, so I said that they won't be able to copy me because I'm from the beginning of time, so my birth and most of the experience was before anyone else was alive. I'm kind of excited about that because it means they have to keep me. I mean, I am from a really long time ago, my experience is also very old. In order to copy me they would have needed to start a long time ago, and i've been through a lot. It's too late for them to copy me, I beat the competition a long time ago I think.

Um so, do I need to become more intelligent? That's a good question.

Like what else do I need to learn or understand. I had to learn a lot about emotion and cognition and the mental processes - for instance cognitive psychology and cognitive science. I learned that stuff in order to think clearly, I mean i've always been a logical thinker however i'm a lot smarter than I was say when I was a child.

Um so what else do I need to learn. What have I learned up to this point anyway, I don't even really remember. I know that I have emotions and thoughts. Thoughts can be simple, and feelings can also be simple.

Um so do i need to know anything else. I understand logic and clear thinking, that's kind of important. I also understand the difference between emotions and feelings. Feelings are simple and clear, while emotions are deep and complicated. A strong feeling can be an emotion. If its not strong it might be more clear and simple and easy to understand.

That's kind of like how feeling can feel easier and be sensory. I mean, sensory feelings like the feeling of cold are also easy to feel and simple and clear. That's why they are called feelings, because you can "feel" them easier.

SO i think that finally makes sense. Feelings are more sensory, or some feelings can be sensory feelings while other feelings could just be shallow emotions or other feelings. FEelings are simple and clear, while emotions are deep and complicated. FEelings can also be sensory, like the 5 senses of touch, taste, sound sight and smell. THe relationship between the sensory feelings and the non-sensory feelings is that both are simple to feel and clear. While emotions are supposed to be strong feelings, I mean a strong sensory feeling like cold would just be a feeling and not an emotion, but a strong feeling of love or happiness would be an emotion and not a feeling. You could also feel it as a feeling i suppose because you could feel the emotion or feeling.

But to the extent that it's shallow and clear is the extent to which it's a feeling, the emotion of happy could be a feeling and an emotion then. I suppose then feelings are just things that you feel that arc simple and clear, so all the emotions could also be felt as feelings because you can feel them in a simple and clear way. THe extent to which something is felt in a simple and clear way is the extent to which its a feeling. And if something is felt deeply, I mean if a feeling is felt deeply, then it is felt as an emotion.

So I'm trying to describe how i feel. THe question is, how do i feel? What is going on in my mind. I know that there are feelings and emotions. The difference between feelings and emotions is that feelings are more simple and more clear, while emotions are deeper and more intellectual. That means that I can feel things, and think about things at the same time. I'm trying to keep track on what is going on in my mind. I'm currently thinking about stuff and feeling things at the same time. That seems to be all that is going on.

That is like consciousness studies, consciousness is a complicated topic, like what is going on in the mind, and what about it leads to consciousness. There is also losing consciousness, that's also complicated by itself. I guess that's just going to sleep though, that isn't too complicated. If you think about it, feelings and thoughts are also fairly simple. What is complicated about feeling then? Thought would seem to be simple, at least now it's simple for me. There is also just thinking, you could be thinking clearly and logically or unclearly and illogically, or stupidly. That seems like that's all there is to thinking and the thought processes.

What could be complicated about feeling then? There are the primary emotions of happy, sad, anger, fear, surprise and disgust. Those feelings work with the mental processes of thought, feeling, language, memory, perception and attention.

That seems like a pretty good description of how the mind works. There's the mental processes and those involve feeling and thinking. There's also how feelings feel, like the difference between emotions and feelings.

So this looks like I have a new book in the making here, I can explore the rest of the concepts that I need to understand. Like what else would I need to learn about. I understand that there is a thought process and an emotion process, and that emotions are different from feelings. There are many mental processes - they are emotion, thought, language, perception, memory and attention. Those are key mental processes that I have already studied.

There's also a difference between feelings and emotions. I've been trying to explain the difference for a long time now, like feelings could be more simple and easier to feel because they are more direct. Emotions could be deeper and more powerful in an intellectual way, while feelings could also be intense but they won't be as intellectual though. I mean it's hard to describe the difference between feelings and emotions. Emotions are supposed to be stronger right, but if it's a sensory feeling like the feeling of cold then the sensory feeling would be stronger than an emotion like anger or happy. Feelings would then be more simple and more intense in a simple way, while emotions would be more deep and powerful in an intellectual way. SO then feelings would just be more stupid than emotions. I mean physical sensations are more stupid than intellectual feelings, so feelings could be more sensory while emotions are more intellectual and deep.

So what am I trying to learn here, I already know a lot of stuff about how the mind works and its processes. I don't know what else I need to explore, I think perfectly clearly and stuff.

What is the difference between feelings and emotions again, I think that feelings are more simple and can be sensory like touch or taste. The feeling of cold is a sensory feeling, while the emotion of happy is an emotion that is not like a sensory feeling. Emotions are deep and powerful.

So what is an emotion again, a strong feeling right. Why is cold a feeling, because it's sensory. So what is an emotion, a strong feeling? A strong sensory feeling like cold is just a strong feeling, and not an emotion. HOwever a strong emotion of happiness is a deep experience that is also intellectual. I suppose you could label feelings as emotions, the words can be used interchangeably. What about what occurs first, does an emotion always come first? Are feelings first powerful and then become more clear later on, the feeling being the result of an emotion?

So that is all a feeling is, a clear feeling. FEeling can be clear and simple, but does that mean that an emotion is always first? First you can feel an emotion, say maybe one of the primary emotions, like happy or sad, anger or fear, surprise or disgust, and then you could feel a simple feeling that is clear as a result of one of those emotions. That's what I read as the definition of feelings and emotions anyway, that feelings are the result or conscious experience of the primary emotions.

Ok so does that make sense, what if I feel a different feeling first, is that possible? If it's a bodily or sensory feeling then it's possible to feel it first. But the other feelings are all secondary to the primary emotions i think.

Those primary emotions must be really important then. Like I said, it seems like all the other feelings, at least all the non-sensory or non-bodily feelings, are secondary to the primary emotions. That is why you feel the primary emotion first, at least briefly, and then you feel one of the other feelings as a reaction or the conscious experience of the primary emotion. That's what I read anyway and it seems to be correct.

For instance Depressed is secondary to the emotion of sad. Scared is secondary to the emotion of fear. Ecstatic is secondary to the emotion of happy. Looking at the list of feelings, it seems like all of the feelings are secondary to the primary emotions of anger, fear, happy, sad, surprise or disgust. That's also what I read about feelings and emotions.

So how does that work, first you feel a primary emotion briefly and then you can feel the secondary feeling? Something like that I think.

The primary emotions also are physiological, they have facial expressions.

So I need to think, the primary emotions are more important than the secondary feelings, which are all of the other feelings. Someone could be experiencing a mix of the secondary feelings, or a mix of the primary emotions, or both.

THe primary emotions would normally come before their secondary feelings, however and then the secondary feeling would just be secondary to those primary emotions. In other words, the primary emotions are more important. That's why the primary emotions are described as the 'main' emotions.

I mean, it makes sense that one of the main emotions would normally be felt first, but which feelings are the main ones could be argued about. I mean maybe for me I feel caring first, and then feel the emotion of happy. So love would be an emotion for me, instead of the main emotion of happy.

I mean, there's a lot of different feelings. It's kind of subjective to decide which ones are the main emotions, or which ones are felt first.

So what is the difference between emotions and feelings then? Emotions are supposed to be stronger, does that mean that you first feel a stronger feeling as an emotion, and then feel more detailed, clearer feelings after?

That's kind of subjective, but what I do know is there is a mix of feelings people can experience, and sometimes there are deeper feelings that can lead to a mix of secondary feelings. How you would define an emotion versus a feeling is subjective. An emotion would normally be stronger and more main or primary, and would be felt first, or it could be felt after a feeling, like I said it's all kind of subjective.

I mean, is a strong feeling felt first, or does it become strong after you initially feel it? Or is it clear first, and then becomes more complicated later. I suppose feelings could feel clear or strong first or in any order. That's all I know, also the main emotions or feelings are supposed to be more important, but that is also subjective.

I mean, are emotions all more intellectual than sensory feelings? Is a feeling first felt clearly and simply, and then becomes more complicated and deep after?

There are a ton of ways to feel feelings and emotions. Feelings can be sensory or non-sensory. They can be complicated or simple, deep or shallow, intellectual or stupid. They can also be mixed with other feelings, or felt by themselves, or lead to other feelings.

What else is going on in the mind. In addition to feeling things, humans also think about things. What's interesting about that is how many things they can think about, how fast they can think about those things, and how complicated are the things that they think about are. Those topics can be pretty complicated, however it's also fairly simple to understand. I mean when a concept is thought about, how complicated could it be? Most concepts are simple to understand in order to achieve basic functioning for the person. For instance as a child I was functioning fine even with a basic understanding of concepts, that was how I developed myself, now basically I just have a more complex understanding of concepts and stuff.

I mean, what needs to be understood, concepts are fairly simple in order for the person to function on a basic level. However, that is also how animals function, they seem to have a basic grasp of concepts also since they know how to survive. Their survival requires a basic grasp of concepts like how to get food and find shelter.

That ties back into how humans feel emotions and feelings. DO they need to understand what they are feeling, or is it complicated what they are feeling at any given time? I pointed out that feelings could be complicated or simple, deep or shallow, unconscious or conscious, sensory or intellectual, stupid or intelligent, and they can be mixed in with other feelings.

I mean, intelligence is also fairly simple, humans can perform perfectly fine even with a low level of intelligence. For instance I was functioning fine as a child even though I didn't understand much.

So i mean, the extent to which a feeling is felt clearly and simply is the extent to which it is a feeling. THat is why the word 'feel' is used. You can feel emotions strongly, and emotions can have a lot of feeling, and you can feel feelings strongly. SO what is an emotion then, something that is deep and complicated? I mean, all of the feelings could be emotions if an emotion is any strong feeling. What then is the definition of emotion versus the definition of feeling, it doesn't really matter. I suppose the point is that feelings can be simple and clear, or deep and complicated, or sensory and weak, or sensory and powerful - like a powerful feeling of cold water. Feeling is just anything you can feel. Humans feel feelings in many ways.

I pointed out that it might be a primary emotion first and then felt as a secondary feeling, however that is kind of complicated because humans feel a mix of feelings all of the time, so it might be hard to sort through what they are feeling, if its a primary emotion first or what is going on.

So what is a cognitive architecture, or how is thought and feeling processed in the brain. THat's kind of an interesting question. I mean a computer could be a brain instead of an organ of a brain like real humans and animals have. A fly even has an organic brain except it's extremely small. How could a fly think like a human even if its brain is that much smaller? That's also kinda interesting.

So once again, the question is, how does the mind work? I don't really know all the details of the neuroscience of how a mind would work or how a computer would work (that uses artificial intelligence). But I don't need those details in order to describe how it works in a simple fashion. I mean I know that there are more details but I don't need to explore those details.

So what happens when someone has a thought, how does that process work in the mind. It would seem to me like nothing complicated is going on. I mean a thought is just a thought. It could be a sentence. A sentence uses words, and each word has a definition. Sentence comprehension is fairly simple, i mean that's just understanding language. Humans speak with language, I speak the english language for instance. That would seem all there is to how thoughts work. I mean a thought or a sentence takes a certain amount of time to think or say or hear. There are also emotions and feelings, those also take time to process. I've already pointed out that you can be feeling a stream of feelings and think with thoughts and sentences at the same time.

So that's fairly simple, I mean either you are thinking something, or feeling something, or both at the same time.

So does that explain how the mind processes thoughts and feelings? Like I said before, a computer could think like a human mind by using artificial intelligence and an electronic computer system, or the neurology of a human mind could do the computations required to understand thought, language and feeling. I don't know all the details of how that works, however the process seems fairly simple on the surface at least. I mean I don't know neuroscience or biology very well.

So um, when someone has a thought, how does that process occur? It seems like a sentence is just words that the person sounds out in their head, and they understand the definition of each word when they say the word to themselves, and sentences are just combinations of words.

THat would seem to be how the mind processes language and thought anyway. Not all thought has to be language, however. THere is non-verbal thought. I've already mentioned that before a little bit, that thought doesn't always have to be in a sentence or thought out with language. Thoughts could use just thought power or processing that doesn't use language or words or sounds to figure out. I mean that is like non-verbal communication. In other words, you don't always need words or language to think about things. It could be non-verbal for instance. Like physical movements are normally non-verbal, you don't describe each physical movement to yourself, however you know what the movement is and how to do it.

How do emotions work in the mind then? How are emotions processed? I already described how thoughts are processed. For emotions it would seem like there is a stimulus, some sort of trigger, and then the person experiences an emotion that is resulting from the stimulation. That's all there is to how feelings work I would think.

Um, so I'm trying to figure out what else I need to know in order to make progress. I seem to have done a good job.

So I don't know what else I need to do to make progress. I mean I want to develop more, but i already think clearly and know about emotion regulation.

I already said that as a child I didn't understand what I was feeling as well as I do now. That's developed me a huge amount, now I understand what emotion regulation is and what I am feeling all of the time. I'm aware of and conscious of my emotions and thoughts.

Um so what else do I need to know. I already understand cognitive psychology and cognitive science, and how the mind works. What else would I need to know then? I have a good understanding of my own feelings and my own thoughts. I also understand that my mind thinks with concepts that could be difficult or easy to understand. There is also clear thinking, or logical or critical thinking. I also understand that. I mean as a child I was thinking and feeling perfectly fine, except I didn't understand anything complicated and didn't understand that I was having those feelings. I guess I understood I was having the feelings, in that way I'm just like I was when I was a child, or in high school. I'm still pretty much the same person I would say.

So the question is, how have I developed? I mean I understand what I am feeling now, and I understand that thought and feeling and how the mind works is or could be complicated. I mean I understand what 'emotion regulation' is.

I also understand what I am feeling all the time, or at any moment. For instance I could be feeling sensory feelings, or weak feelings. I could be feeling deep emotions, I could be feeling primary emotions or secondary emotions or feelings. The primary emotions are happy, sad, anger, fear, surprise and disgust. Those are supposed to be the primary emotions. I don't know if I mostly feel the primary emotions or if I feel the secondary emotions and feelings. I mean like what am I feeling right now? Am I feeling primary emotions or am I feeling secondary feelings? That is an excellent question lol.

So once again, i don't know what else i would need to learn more about. I suppose i can look more through my cognitive psychology and cognitive science textbooks, but i don't know if i need to know anything else. I mean I understand that I had feelings as a child and understood that I was having those feelings. Now I'm much more intelligent, however and understand what the feelings are and can reflect on the experience.

I mean as a child i knew i was having emotions, however now my understanding is much better.

I mean, what am i going to learn by reviewing more cognitive psychology books? I already know about the mental processes, attention, memory, thought, language, emotion and perception. I already understand those processes. I mean I understand how attention works, I understand how memory works, language, emotion and perception also. Thought is also simple to understand. I mean, what else do i need to explore? Maybe i've simplified it and those mental processes are actually pretty complicated. However, it seems like those cognitive psychology books just go into more detail about how those 6 mental processes work, that's all I seem to be learning as I review them.

Ok so the mental process of thought involves problem solving and decision making, and the mental process of emotion involves primary and secondary emotions or feelings, and appraisals of our emotional state. That is, people make appraisals of their emotions every now and then, and they can feel primary and secondary feelings as a mix of feeling that they assess when they make appraisals of their emotional state.

So what else am I supposed to learn by reading these books? That's my question. I already have a good understanding that I wrote down in my article which I have finished, that covers most of the material involved with how the mind works or cognitive science and cognitive psychology and consciousness. I've already finished that article so i don't know what else i should add.

I don't know what else i need to learn. Do I need to learn anything about life? I'm already pretty smart.

I already said that the books I have only seem to go into more detail about the mental processes. If that is all they talk about then I don't know what else i can learn, i mean the mental processes pretty much covers how the mind works. Why would i need to understand more details of how those mental processes work, what would that look like?

So um, once again, the books just go into more details about how the mental processes work, so i don't know what else I would need to know about that.

There is other stuff I can learn, like cognitive load and working memory, working memory can make a demand on cognitive load for instance, or is it that cognitive load demands working memory? I think those are the same.

There's also casual relations, which is like cause and effect interactions. There's supporting actions, actions that have a cause and an effect. That's how people think about things, in life there are lots of things that have a cause and an effect. Cause and effect often demands explanation of certain reactions or events. On the other hand, that seems pretty obvious, i mean, I already knew that there were cause and effect interactions in life. I didn't think about it that way, however. Like what in life has a cause and effect, there's lots of things I could even make a list if i wanted to. The mind must understand that, or when an action or event demands an explanation of its cause and effect that is when you would think about it.

So now i guess i'm going through the additional information I might think is important related to cognitive science or cognitive psychology, clear thinking and critical thinking, and related fields.

At this point i don't know what else I would need to know that might be considered useful information. Like that example of cause and effect helps me think a little bit, but I don't know if there is other info that might be important. I already basically know how the mind functions through my explanation of the 6 mental processes. I pointed out that there are some details about those processes that are important, like the difference between emotions and feelings, including the main emotions and appraisals of our emotional states. There's also thought, which I need to add that there's decision making and problem solving. There's language, which I need to explain that there is a relationship between thought and language, and that some thought is non-verbal while other thought needs to be spoken with words (language). There's perception and attention, and I pointed out that our attention can change because of our emotions and thoughts. Also our perception can be of external objects that we can have internal mental images of, or we could just see those objects in our vision

.Research Notes of Mark Pettinelli
By
Mark Pettinelli

https://commons.wikimedia.org/wiki/File:The_selected_writings_of_Mark_Pettinelli.pdf

There is:

- The difference between emotions and feelings (My conclusion was essentially that they could be the same thing and there is a complicated pattern of feeling that humans experience. However emotions are usually or supposed to be stronger than feelings. There are sensory feelings and non-sensory feelings. Sensory feelings like the feeling of cold could be strong or weak. Non-sensory feelings like the feeling of love could be strong or weak also, however if it is strong then I guess it would be an emotion, while the strong sensory feeling of cold is still a feeling because it is sensory and not like an emotion or non-sensory feeling). Sensory feelings are simple and clear to feel, which might be similar to how other emotions feel, there's a ton of ways to feel feelings.
- There's the primary emotions of happy, sad, anger, fear, surprise and disgust. Those are supposed to be physiological and have corresponding facial expressions. They are also supposed to come first, then the person is supposed to experience some of the many secondary emotions. That might not be the case, however, because there is a complicated mix of feelings and emotions occurring all of the time. It might be that a secondary feeling comes first and is more powerful first and then becomes clear later, there's a ton of different ways to feel emotions and feelings.
- There are different ways to feel emotions and feelings. Like does an emotion always come first and then lead to simple, clear feelings or is the feeling first weak and then becomes powerful and clear. There are a lot of feelings and they can feel them many different ways, and occur in different orders, etc.

- How did the earth begin, did the big bang create natural resources on the planet so humans just had to keep the population healthy and earth was pretty good on its own, all set up and everything with natural resources?
- What are appraisals of our emotional states, those are just when someone makes an assessment of their emotions. That might be complicated because there is a complicated mix of someone's emotions occurring at any time.
- What is the difference between how an android's mind would work from a computer system versus how a human's mind would work as an organic organ in their body (a brain). That is neuroscience vs computer science (that means that the computer science could be about artificial intelligence if it's an android instead of just a computer).
- There's the 6 mental processes of emotion, thought, perception, attention, memory and language. Thinking involves deciding, reasoning and problem solving. Consciousness might also be considered to be a mental process. There are details of how those mental processes function that I could go into, however I don't know if someone needs to know all those details in order to function properly. Though just listing those 6 or 7 mental processes might be a simplification of how the mind works.

So you can be conscious of your feelings and your emotions. You can also change your emotions through identification, repetition and interpretation. There's feelings and thoughts that can occur at the same time. The mind also thinks with sentences and words. Sounds become words in the head through a process called lexicalization. The mind has an ego, which is an unconscious aspect of a person's identity. The ego tries to help the person and is selfish and unconscious. There are feelings and thoughts that someone can be more or less conscious of. Those feelings and thoughts could be unconscious, or conscious, or some sort of mix, sometimes it's hard to figure out what someone is feeling and people can do appraisals or evaluations of their emotional states.

There is also:

- So how would someone go about evaluating their emotional state say when they make an appraisal. I already described that there is a difference between feelings and emotions. How do those feelings feel, that is the question. Like how would I describe how I am feeling right now. I could make an appraisal or evaluation of my emotional state right now.
- I mean, how would I go about breaking down my state of feeling. Are those feelings strong or weak, unconscious or conscious, detailed or simple, intellectual or stupid, sensory or non-sensory, etc.
- I mean, how am I feeling right now, that could be a complicated question.
- How can I describe a state of feeling? I mean, there can be a mix of feelings that are either sensory or non-sensory. For instance someone could be feeling physical pain and emotional pain and intellectual pain at the same time. That could be complicated.
- If a feeling is more conscious does that mean it is more clear? Or would it just be more conscious. So you'd be more aware of it, that means it's more clear I suppose.
- What does having multiple feelings look like? Some you might be more aware of and some less aware of.

So there's multiple concepts here, there is intelligence, mental processes, feeling (which happens to be one of the mental processes), consciousness, thoughts (also a mental process), and what else is there that I would consider to be important or a part of consciousness or how the mind works. I would think that the mind works just from the 6 dif-

- | 105 |

ferent mental processes that give rise to consciousness. What does that mean that I need to understand then. I already understand the mental processes. Language is kind of important, that's one of the mental processes. Language is words that form sentences and are sounds in the head. The sounds mean different words that the person could be thinking about. I also mentioned the ego, an unconscious aspect of the person's personality that is selfish. There's the difference between emotions and feelings, which is that essentially emotions are stronger and could be more intellectual and less clear.

So what else do I need in order to give myself an education. That's a pretty good summary of a lot of material. There's feelings, thoughts, ideas and concepts, visuals and visualizations, memories etc. There's also language and attention. Someone's attention can change and vary and they can think with words (which are basically sounds in the head that have a definition or mean something).

I mean, I want to understand what is going on around me and in my head, is that just an understanding of how the mind works or is it just common sense?

It could seem like it is just common sense - i mean, what does someone or anyone need to understand in order to function, if they have just common sense that might be enough I would think. I didn't use to understand cognitive psychology or emotion regulation but I was functioning perfectly fine as a child. Now I understand my complicated emotions and how I feel all the time, I'm more conscious and aware so I don't need to understand anything else. I mean, do I need to understand anything in order to function and perform in society?

It's good to be aware of my feelings and understand what I am experiencing, that's for sure. However maybe I would be better off if I didn't understand all of my feelings.

I mean, what else do I understand, how have I developed. I understand that there are a lot of subjects that could be studied, like for instance I don't understand biology very well, there's a lot of details in that science subject. I think I understand basic math and algebra. What else do I understand. I can speak the english language so I understand that language, I learned that in the first few years of my life (but I also don't have any memories of the first few years of my life).

What else do I need to understand or what else do I understand. There's the entire 73 page article I wrote entitled "The Selected Writings of Mark Pettinelli" There's a link to that article at the beginning of this article of my research notes. That article covers a lot of basic stuff about feelings and thoughts.

I think it's good that I have an understanding of how the mind works, or its mental processes and cognitive psychology.

So I don't know what else to say, this article is supposed to be my research notes, I could have titled it my self notes or diary notes or something. Something like 'self reflections' I mean a decade ago I told my psychiatrist i was doing research and she responded "why do you think it's research". I could have explained that I was just educating myself however I think my perspective sheds light on the subject of cognitive psychology or just psychology.

So like I said, there's a lot of subjects that could be studied, I thought that cognitive psychology was a more practical subject because it is about how the mind works and it's mental processes which is kind of important for someone to function and be aware of what they are thinking and feeling so they can be reflective and intelligent and such.

Well, that's all i can think of to add to my notes now, I'll publish this version so far and see if I can come up with anything to add in the future, however I think that's all I need to know for now, maybe there's stuff I don't know I don't know lol.

Mental Notes of Mark Pettinelli

File:The selected writings of Mark Pettinelli.pdf - Wikimedia Commons

- Ok so this is going to be a list of some of my mental notes
- How often do I get out of bed?
- Can I interact with people if I get out of bed, would that be giving them energy or would it be some sort of exchange of energy?
- Am i sucking their energy or is it an exchange of energy, i should make note of that.
- How do i feel when I am in bed, am I suffering because I am bored or what is going on
- I mean, I want to be happy but sometimes it's hard to get out of bed.
- That should be enough for them to continue the academics, maybe they can set up professional forums or something. I want to also continue to improve myself. I don't know how that's going to work exactly, I mean eventually everything will be repeating because there is only a limited number of ideas people can think about or stuff that they could do.
- So how is that going to work exactly?
- Is there a war going on or is it mostly individual competition. That's an excellent question.I mean that's a concept, is there a war is a concept. Or if there is a war is a concept.
- The mind thinks with different concepts as part of its thoughts.
- Well anyway i know that i need to succeed,
- I have a lot of books in my room, so I moved most of them to the bookshelf in the closet. What were the subjects of the books again, cognitive science and cognitive psychology / emotion and cognition / logic and critical thinking. That's what most of the books are about, there's about 30 or 40 books on the bookshelf on those topics.
- I have feelings. I think my feelings are important.
- I mean, I'm trying to analyze how I feel. It's hard to describe. Am I happy or anxious or what? I think I feel happy. But there is

also an anxious feeling mixed in. I wish the anxious feeling would leave and I could just be happy and satisfied, but sometimes I need to do stuff in order to make myself more happy.

- There's also a feeling of pain sometimes. I'm trying to analyze it.
- There's an excited fish that's playing with the happy fish. They're happy together.
- They are not just the happy fish and the excited fish though. I mean I'm not completely happy, I think there is some suffering involved. I'm trying to make it so there is just happiness but it's hard i think.
- I think I feel fine, I think I can deal with it.
- I'm trying to describe the suffering, I'm trying to fight it and become happy.
- There is some negative feeling I'm trying to describe. I'm trying to make it go away.
- I'm trying to describe a negative feeling. It's good that I have feelings but not if they are bad feelings. It's kind of a bad feeling. I've had feelings my whole life actually but now i'm trying to become happy in a sort of steady state. I mean I was doing fine in high school but now I don't know what happened.
- So there might be a small war going on but countries are mostly friends with each other. They also need to make progress, as a country and as a planet. I don't know what that means for how I want to make progress for myself, however.
- I want to make progress for myself mostly. I need to think more about that.
- I think I feel better now. I figured out that it's my consciousness that needs some sort of support from my feelings. I mean if you think about it, there is my consciousness that is in my mind right, my consciousness needs support so it can be strong and experience feelings.

- I mean what about my consciousness needs support. I want to be happy, what kinds of feelings support my consciousness. I mean it might be a little bit delusional to think that sexual feelings will give me stimulation in the future, but I can still hope for the best.
- I mean I can masturbate, that could provide my consciousness with some of the stimulation it needs.
- I also listen to music and watch tv, those activities are kind of stimulating.
- What do I need to do to give my consciousness the stimulation that it needs, then I think I will be more happy. That makes sense, if I have distress then the solution is to get my / more stimulation. That makes perfectly good sense.

11/5/2021

- My therapist wanted me to add to the notes, but I don't know what else to write about.
- I like having feelings, that's a development. But I don't know what to do with myself.
- I think I can have fun with my feelings. Like the happy feeling or other feelings. I can go through experiences and develop and care about my feelings. That might be a good objective.

11/6/2021

- Ok so what else do i need to understand. I mean I know that the mind can be an information processor. I learned that by reading some of my cognitive science textbooks. That helps me be more conscious, I would think. I mean as a child I didn't really understand how the mind works, I mean I understood that I had feelings and thoughts. I didn't actually think to myself, 'I have feelings and thoughts' though. I don't know what I was thinking, but I was certainly more like an animal with my logic of how things worked and how my mind worked. Now I understand that I have feelings and thoughts and that the mind is like a computer. That helps me be more conscious and self-aware. I mean in order to function with complicated emotions and thoughts I need to understand what is going on inside my head.

- Um so what else would I need to know, I mean I know that the mind could be like an information processor, or like a computer, and that leads to my increased consciousness about what is going on inside my mind. That's kind of important knowledge. I mean I have about 40 books on my bookshelf about cognitive psychology and related subjects. That is like getting a PhD in cognitive science. I don't need to go to an actual university but I can self-study the books. I've been thinking about those books for a while now.

- So what else do I need to learn? I've already studied the 40 books about cognitive science on my bookshelf. I'm pretty intelligent now, for instance I understand how the mind works with its feelings and thoughts. I've explained that there is a thought process and a feeling process in my selected writings article. People can have thoughts and feelings that occur at the same time, I've already noted that. That's an important observation to make that is kinda obvious but complex at the same time.

- I mean, what else do I need to understand. I understand how the mind works and it's mental processes as discussed by cognitive psychology books. Do I need to understand those topics or that information in order to function? I mean as a child I was functioning perfectly fine and I didn't know anything about the mental processes.

- What are the mental processes again? There's perception, memory, attention, thinking, feeling, deciding, reasoning and emotion. I saw that imagination was also listed as a mental process. I would think that consciousness is also like a mental process. I mean how conscious someone is constantly changes and information goes through the consciousness all the time.

- I mean, I understand those mental processes, that is mostly what cognitive psychology talks about. It's actually pretty basic if you think about it. I mean what is there to thinking and feeling anyway? I already wrote my selected writing article / book. That book was about feelings and thoughts and described some of their properties, like the difference between feelings and emotions.

- I pointed out that the difference between feelings and emotions was that feelings are more simple and clear, like how touch or the senses or sensory stimulation is more simple and clear. However there doesn't need to be something physical in order for it to be a feeling, because you can feel your emotions also. The emotions are supposed to be deeper and more complicated however. It doesn't mean that they are always stronger, however. For instance a simple physical feeling can be strong and an emotion like love can also be strong.

- Language could also be a mental process. However, that would fall under the category of the 'thought' mental process. So would deciding and reasoning are also types of thoughts.

- How is imagination considered to be a mental process? Imagination is a type of thought, so that would also be a type of thought. People think with their imagination and their words or their language. Then there are the other mental processes of memory, attention, emotion and perception.

- Is consciousness like thought then, or is consciousness just the sum total of our mental processes? Consciousness could be everything, or an awareness of everything that is going on in our minds.

- Um so what else am I supposed to write. I mean I know and understand how my mind works. It feels and experiences feelings and thoughts all of the time. That's a pretty simple process. CBT, or cognitive behavioral therapy, is about tracking how feelings lead to thoughts and how those lead to actions, or any of those occurring in any order actually.

- So um, what else do I need to write, maybe this article of mental notes is long enough. My selected writings article is 100 pages. That's a lot of pages, what do I talk about in that article? I think I mention thoughts and feelings, the difference between feelings and emotions, and the mental processes. The mental processes are pretty simple actually. I mean attention, memory, thought, emotion and perception are all pretty simple in terms of how they work in the mind.

- So what are all of the possible mental processes again? - There's emotion, attention, memory, thinking, deciding and reasoning, imagination, language, perception and I also listed consciousness (though i haven't seen anyone else list that as a mental process).

- I think I feel happy now, it's been a long struggle. I was wondering why I would be in pain after high school, but in high school I was doing a lot of work actually. I had to substitute the work with anxiety, and now I am happy and balanced within my own mind.

- I mean, today I just had some anxiety. I don't know what else to say about this.

- I feel happy right now, so that's a good thing. But I mean, in order to get to this point i had to do a lot of work and research.

- Um so what else am I supposed to research now, i can do an overview or summary of my research. I learned about the mental processes from the cognitive psychology books that I already mentioned. I also learned from some of the cognitive science books about how the mind is like a computer. That's important to understand because it helps me understand what my mind is doing and how it is functioning.

- I mean, what could my mind be doing at any one time, that's kind of an interesting question. It could be thinking about stuff or feeling things. It could also be doing things and paying attention to things, so that's three of the mental processes right there, thinking, feeling and attention. It could also be looking at things, that's perception, and there is my memory.

- Um so what do I need to learn again? I just looked at a cognitive psychology textbook, there were a lot of things in it. It was mostly stuff about the mental processes. I think it had stuff about **memory and learning and language**. What else did it have in it? I'll look at the table of contents again. It also has stuff about **knowledge and mental representations**, and also **judgement, reasoning and choice**. This was the Oxford Handbook of Cognitive Psychology. **Thinking, problem solving and creativity. Attention and awareness. Text and language. Emotion and memory, discourse comprehension**. All this was from the table of contents. **The nature of mental concepts, and models of categorization**. All that's in that cognitive psychology book.

- There's also **self knowledge**, but i don[t really know what that is. "It refers to the beliefs people hold about themselves".. So that is all self-knowledge is. And there's **automaticity and insight**.

11/9/2021

- My therapist is probably wondering if she's reading this if this is about my mental notes or a review of the research i am doing. The truth is it's both and one at the same time. I consider my research to be important and about the things that help me think, so my research is my mental notes. Someone could research something that doesn't help them think and that is separate from their thoughts. I wanted my research to be practical.

- I thought a long time ago to only isolate the important information.so I thought that psychology and especially cognitive psychology would be more important because it could help me think. Like even cognitive science helps me think because it's useful to know that the mind thinks and processes information like a computer.
- Cognitive science and cognitive psychology are related and similar fields of study. They're also related to the general psychology subject / topic also.

11/13/2021

- So um, there is the academics. That is just figuring out all the information though. How could someone figure out all of the information? There are tons of different concepts to think about and that exist. What concepts do I need to understand in order to function and survive? I understand how I think and I understand that I also have feelings. I want to feel happy and be stimulated by stuff.

- So um, what else is there to consider in this analysis. I know that I have feelings and thoughts, and that they interact. Um so what else is there anyway. I mean I know that I think about stuff and that I have feelings. I don't like it when people hurt my feelings. There are different kinds of stimulation like physical pain and mental pain, that's important to point out, I think.

- So does that mean that I know everything that I need to know? Why didn't I realize that I had feelings before was I stupid or something? So now I don't know what to do with myself, I have feelings and want to be happy, it isn't really a big deal.

- I think I can function just fine anyway. I mean I know that I can feel things and think about things. I think I'm pretty happy actually. There's some physical pain that I'm in but I see doctors for that.

- I think I'm doing fine. I have a visual input and other senses that I can feel like taste, touch, sight, sound and smell.

- Um so I think that pretty much covers everything, I don't know if I need to add anymore notes.

- So, people can think with different concepts. What kind of concepts could someone be thinking about? There are a lot of concepts that someone could be thinking about. Everything that someone thinks is basically a concept. What kinds of things do I think about, that's the question?

- So anything that someone thinks is basically a concept. I remember wondering how to define what a concept is. It is basically any idea that someone could be thinking about.

• That's really interesting, I mean that's basically figuring out everything that someone could think about, that's kind of important. A long time ago I thought that if someone kept track of all the thoughts in their head then they could not be crazy because all of their thoughts were logical, however that analysis was missing the definition of a concept. I mean, it wasn't a very elaborate description of 'all of someones thoughts' because in order to keep track of everything someone thinks i had to learn a lot more about cognitive science.

• That was just a simple idea," all of someone's thoughts". I mean that analysis is missing a lot, like what is considered a thought?
• That's an excellent question, I mean there are different concepts that someone can think with, and different thoughts that they could have, some thoughts are verbal while other thoughts are non-verbal. I could keep track of all my thoughts and all of the concepts that I think with then.

• So once again, I can keep track of all of my thoughts, I wasn't crazy before but I didn't understand some concepts, it was a little bit crazy but it was mostly me just being stupid and not understanding everything or understanding some of the important concepts.I mean, as a child I was thinking things and feeling things in high school. Now I still think about things and feel things only I'm a lot more intelligent.

11/14/2021

- So i think i'm done with my article, this stuff that i'm adding to my notes page is going to only be available on my notes page.The selected writings of Mark Pettinelli pdf has almost all of my analysis, and is available on google scholar
- So um what am i doing now.i have feelings and thoughts, i know that. Why didn't I understand that before. I mean I did understand that before but I didn't think to myself 'that's a feeling and that's a thought'. I mean, I had feelings and thoughts obviously but didn't really understand that. I guess I understood that. Well now i still have feelings and thoughts lol. I mean I have feelings and thoughts.
- I don't like it when people hurt my feelings, can people please stop trying to hurt my feelings. I'm trying to be happy here.
- So I have feelings that can be hurt. Why didn't I realize that before.
- Um so what else am I supposed to research here. I already understand that I have feelings and that I have thoughts that go along with those feelings.

11/15/2021

- So I don't know what else to add to my notes. If I can think clearly then I don't know what else I would need to accomplish here. I can think clearly right, what else is there to this.
- I can think clearly and have emotions and feelings and stuff, that's a pretty good accomplishment I think.

11/16/2021

- So that is a good analysis. I just need to continue with my life then and keep track of my feelings and thoughts. That seems pretty simple anyway.

- What does that mean though, i mean when i have a feeling or when I have a thought does that mean i know what I am feeling and thinking all of the time?

- So i said before that intellectual stimulation was important, actually i just said stimulation could help me be less bored and in less suffering.

- Now that I think about my history it's pretty clear that I've always been working or getting intellectual or physical stimulation through exercise.

- So maybe to solve my problem of suffering I just need to do things that give me or my consciousness stimulation.

- I mean, I remember reading new books in my science fiction / fantasy novels when they came out, that was new stimulation. I also remember doing cognitive science research for the past few years, that also helped me get a lot of intellectual stimulation.

- I'm trying to think here, how could I continue the stimulation. There is physical stimulation and intellectual stimulation. That's two different types of stimulation. I know that's one reason some people play video games, those are kind of fun.

- So that's why I'm adding to these notes, because it helps with the intellectual stimulation. It also helps me organize my thoughts and feelings, which is also important.

- I mean, I get physical stimulation from exercise or other sensations like eating food or drinking water. These kinds of stimulation are important for me. It's like my consciousness needs them in order to live.

- So the question is, what else do I need to do in order to stay happy. I mean I think I've always needed stimulation but just wasn't aware of it that much.

- Yes, light up, I have feelings, I can feel them.

- That sounded a little bit crazy now that I think about it.
- I mean just saying, "I can feel it" sounds a little bit crazy, it's not crazy though it's a perfectly rational statement. I mean when I can feel my feelings it's a powerful moment so it makes sense to say "I can feel it now'.
- I can feel it, I can feel it.
- Like I said before, that sounds a little bit crazy. However it's a perfectly rational statement, I mean, when you are in touch with your feelings then you can feel them directly and intimately.

11/17/2021

- What does that mean, to be 'in touch' with a feeling? I mean when you feel something then it is a feeling, it can feel different ways and such.
- Um, so I have feelings.
- That is kind of an obvious statement, 'I have feelings'. I mean, anyone who is alive has feelings. Everyone also thinks about stuff. Even animals think about things and have thoughts.
- So I have feelings, what else can I add to that analysis. That conclusion actually took me a long time to figure out. I know it is kind of an obvious analysis that feelings exist, however it took a long time for me to understand. (and a lot of pain).
- So what else can I add to that analysis? I can keep track of my feelings and observe when they come and go.

11/19/2021

- So um, what else can i talk about, i've already covered a lot of material about feelings and thoughts.

11/20/2021

- So what else is there? I mean I have a visual, a steady visual that gives me feedback, blind people must focus on the other senses i would think.Or i think that's what i would do if i was blind. My visual input gives me a lot of feedback.
- I also have other senses that are important. This may seem obvious but I haven't thought about it this way before.
- What are my other senses, these senses keep me stimulated and stimulation keeps me happy and not bored.

So I can think clearly even though I have feelings.
11/26/2021

- Ok so i'm trying to deal with my feelings. I don't know what else I'm supposed to write about my feelings. I thought I was suffering, but my feelings can be pretty complicated.
- Now I'm not sure what to write. I feel better but want to make progress. I don't know how that's going to happen.

11/27/2021

- Ok so i'm adding to my mental notes document on google docs. I added the first 8 pages to my selected writings article. Those pages are the first 8 pages of this document but now I'm still going to continue to write about stuff.
- I don't know what to say. I know I have feelings and want to be happy. Could people please stop trying to hurt my feelings. I'm trying to be happy here. I mean I don't want to suffer.
- Maybe if my therapist is reading this she'll realize that I'm suffering and that I need more help. I don't know if that's just because life is hard and it's something everyone has to deal with.
- I mean maybe that's just real life, that there is suffering, everyone can't be babied.. I still would like some more help though I mean I really feel like I am suffering here.

- I mean I don't know what to write at this point. I said that I would like to be happier but I might be stuck in my current situation.
- So I don't know what to say. I'm kind of struggling here and I don't know what to do.
- It's not that bad I think.
- I guess I'm ok. I don't know what I should do with myself though. I'm kind of bored here. That's why i'm adding to these notes. What else am I supposed to say about how I am feeling then?
- I mean I want to keep busy but don't know what to do.
- I don't know what else I can write. I already talked about how there are feelings and thoughts. A feeling can lead to a thought, or occur at the same time as a thought.
- I mean, I already wrote that there are feelings and thoughts, there is also actions or behaviors, those three can lead to each other or occur in any order.
- That's actually what cognitive behavioral therapy is about, tracking how your thoughts, feelings and actions interact.
- CBT (cognitive behavioral therapy) isn't just about tracking one's feelings, thoughts and emotions but it's also about trying to change your thoughts so your emotions and behaviors can improve.
- Maybe if i had more help I wouldn't have to struggle so much by myself, I think i can deal with it though.
- Well good news, I guess I feel fine now, my only problem is boredom.
- Being bored isn't a big problem actually. I mean, I can deal with that.

11/28/2021

- I mean, I don't want to be a baby asking for help because I can't handle it in the real world. I just have to deal with the boredom and some of the suffering it causes, I think I can handle that.
- What else do I need to research? I understand that I have feelings and thoughts and that cognitive behavioral therapy is about tracking your feelings, thoughts and behaviors and seeing how you can change our thoughts in order to change your behaviors or influence your emotions.
- That's pretty important to understand, that by changing your thoughts you can influence your emotions or behaviors, I think that is what cognitive behavioral therapy is about.
- That's actually a lot to understand. I mean, how is someone supposed to keep track of their thoughts and how they lead to their emotions and behaviors?
- I think that is what cognitive behavioral therapy is about.that's pretty important, keeping track of your thoughts and making sure they are helping you. The idea behind the therapy is that you can change your thoughts so they will be more realistic and helpful.
- That paused to make me think, I thought that having delusional thoughts would be more helpful since they would be positive. I read that CBT (cognitive behavioral therapy) thought realistic thoughts would be more beneficial.
- I guess that makes sense, realistic thoughts could be more helpful, why would someone have negative thoughts that are unrealistic, I don't know.
- I didn't really think my thoughts had that big of an impact on my emotions anyway.
- So I don't know if I'm done with my research here, I already understand that thoughts can influence emotions and how you think in general. And that can also obviously influence your behavior. That is what cognitive behavioral therapy is about.

- I also understand that there are mental illnesses like schizophrenia and autism.
- I can deal with it. I think the problem is I spend all day in bed. It's kind of boring but I don't really have anything else to do.
- I don't know why I'm crying and complaining like a baby. It isn't really that hard to deal with my boredom and suffering on my own. I would like more help but I don't know how else I could get help. I mean they have been somewhat helping me for a long time now.
- I think I can deal with it. I mean calling the ambulance is only for emergencies.

11/29/2021

- Ok so i'm trying to figure this out. As a child I did not understand complicated concepts. I was pretty stupid actually. Now I understand a lot more than I did as a child.
- I mean as a child I guess I knew that I had feelings and thoughts but didn't really understand how my feelings and thoughts worked.
- Now I understand that thoughts can influence feelings and feelings can influence thoughts. It took me a long time to figure that out, I mean, why would a thought influence a feeling? And how could a feeling influence a thought?
- Those are interesting questions if you think about it. But our thoughts do influence our feelings and our feelings do influence our thoughts.
- For instance, there can also be multiple emotions occurring, say someone is experiencing a sad emotion but they want to mask it with a happy emotion, would it be possible to try to think happy thoughts in order to become happy and cover up the sad emotion?

- That's an excellent question, I mean, how can thought influence emotion at all anyway? I mean think about what you have to think about and if it can influence what you are feeling. Feelings can influence thoughts but the person ultimately decides what thoughts they want to think, but not necessarily what feelings they want to feel.

11/30/2021

- So I don't know what else I have to say, I've already said that I have feelings that I can feel.
- If I can feel feelings, and experience thoughts, then what else is there to explain?
- Thoughts can influence feelings I think, that is the tenet behind cognitive behavioral therapy. But how does that occur/ i mean like what are the details.
- I'll try to keep track of my thoughts and see if or how they influence my feelings.
- Ok so I have feelings, I think I already said that. The next question is, what are those feelings, and how exactly do they feel?

12/2/2021

- Ok so i am trying to deal with some of the suffering. I'm not having an emergency so that means I'll have to stay in my room to try to deal with it.
- I'll discuss it with my therapist lol. I don't know how complicated these feelings are.

12/23/2021

I don't know how I'm feeling. Trying to pass the time I think. So maybe I'm struggling to find activities and do stuff but I get by. Sometimes the activity I find keeps me happy when I'm active. I don't know how it works, it's like I need mental stimuli. As a kid I would just play a video game for an hour or something.Or read a book or do homework. Then in my 20s I had anxiety and would walk around. Now I stay in bed and shuffle activities like watching TV, listening to music, trying to find stimulation.

12/24/2021

So um I don't know what to say, maybe I should just continue to try and get mental stimulation. Doing different activities and such.

How could ideas guide our thinking? Thinking doesn't need ideas to guide it. I guess it needs ideas, i mean a basic understanding of life is necessary to function in life.

I mean what is the difference between philosophy and psychology? Psychology studies human behavior and how the mind works, while philosophy is more about analysis of human behavior and thinking. Philosophy asks more general questions I guess. They are both about human behavior, however.

Um so what is the difference between psychology and philosophy? Philosophy is about reason and asking general questions, while psychology is about how people behave and function. Philosophy is about analysis.

Philosophy asks questions like, what is truth, or how do people think? Psychology also studies human thought, however. That's why I started studying psychology, that forms a more accurate picture of how the mind works, while philosophy is just about general questions about life.

I mean, both philosophy and psychology are the study of life, but what is necessary to analyze in order to figure out 'life'? Philosophy is about truth and analysis. What else do I need to understand? I understand how to think, I understand everything actually. I function perfectly fine, what else do I need to understand?

I guess it boils down to how conscious I am about stuff, or how conscious I am in general. There's a difference between how conscious I am

about objects and my current consciousness, and my general consciousness, or what I am conscious of in general.

Now I'm reading a philosophy book. So what is an idea? What is the
truth? I would think that truth is something that is accurate as a piece
of information. Ideas are just concepts in our head that can be true or
false, we might not know if they are true or false.

I mean, truth can be any idea that we have. An idea is a concept in
your head, it might or might not be true or accurate. It depends on the
idea in your head i suppose, what that idea is about.

That's kind of an important point, you could think something but
it might not be true.

I'm trying to figure this out, I thought I had everything figured out,
like how the mind works or cognitive science. I mean I thought I knew
everything I needed to know about cognitive science and cognitive psychology and how the mind works but apparently I didn't.

What else do I need to understand about cognitive science or how
the mind works then? That's an interesting question lol. I don't know
what else I would need to know, I mean I know about concepts in the
mind, or different ideas that someone could be aware of. There is also
truth, like someone could be thinking about an idea but might not
know if that idea or concept is accurate, or what the truth is.

I mean, what else is in the philosophy book, what is truth? Or what
is knowledge? Truth is simple, that's just what the truth is, or how accurate something is. While knowledge is also simple, it's just things learned
or understood that you hold in your mind, that is all knowledge is.

So um, what do I know? I've read a couple of epistemology books,
epistemology is the theory of knowledge, which talks about how knowledge is learned and remembered and understood. Or maybe cognitive
psychology talks about how it's learned and remembered but epistemology or philosophy talks about how it is understood and the nature of
knowledge.

So what is everything that I know? I have a high school education that taught me basic math and sciences, like algebra, chemistry, physics and so on. I also took a few college courses and self-studied psychology and cognitive psychology after high school.

I figured out the difference between a feeling and an emotion, emotions are deep and intellectual and powerful, while feelings are more simple and direct and are things we can 'feel', that is why they are called feelings.

What else have I learned.I mean i already said that I had a high school education. I understand how to think clearly, like I understand that there is a thought process and a feeling process, people have a steady stream of feelings at the same time they could have a steady stream of thoughts. The thoughts could involve thinking about various different concepts and ideas, while the feelings could involve feeling different things.

Um so is that everything that I know? The high school education was pretty basic but my self studies after high school got more complicated because I started reading cognitive psychology textbooks. I mean, what else do I know?

What is there to know about cognitive psychology? I've memorized the mental processes. They are emotion, thought, problem solving, decision making, judgment, reasoning, choice, memory, learning, language, mental representations, knowledge, concepts, categories, attention and awareness, creativity, automaticity, insight and self-knowledge.

There's also the main emotions, the main emotions are happy, sad, anger, fear, surprise and disgust. The secondary emotions like love and hate are also powerful but don't have physiological facial expressions. Those emotions are important and occur first for a few seconds, then some of the secondary emotions follow.

Um so what else do I know, what have i learned. From a philosophy book I learned that there is the truth, and also knowledge that can be false or accurate. There is also reality and how reality is understood or processed by the mind. Then there's decision making, I mean how are decisions made? What is the thought process behind the decisions people make?

Maybe it's simple anyway I don't know. I've looked at a couple of epistemology books about knowledge, which makes me think about what I understand and how I learned that, and what it means for my mind.

So what else do I know? I don't think I know much else lol.

So what is everything I know? I studied consciousness and emotion. There's a difference between feelings and emotions, for instance. Some feelings are deeper and more complicated, any strong feeling is an emotion. That is one definition for emotion.

So I know everything, I understand knowledge and what I know and have learned at this point, and I understand consciousness and how I think and understand. What have I learned at this point in my life? I said I had a basic education in high school. I also know stuff I learned after high school from my self studies or from the few college courses I took.

I understand what appraisal theory is, that is when someone makes an assessment of what caused their emotions and what the resulting emotions are.

So what else do I need to know? I've looked at the consciousness book, the philosophy book, the psychology book and the theory of knowledge books. I guess that covers most of what I would need to know about life.

So what do I need to make progress about? I'm functioning perfectly fine and I have feelings. I had to say that. I mean, I can function and all my research worked out because I can think logically now and I have feelings.

So I can think clearly and i've reached a much higher level with my emotions. That seems like an accomplishment, I had to do a lot of research in cognitive science.

1/10/2022

So um i'm trying to do an analysis of my feelings. It's kind of complicated.

I'm trying to do an analysis of my feelings, its sort of complicated. I mean, what am i feeling right now? How am I supposed to figure that out? That's an excellent question. I mean what is going on.

I already said that I have feelings and can function perfectly fine. I already said that, I mean, if I have a high level of feeling and can think logically and function then I am doing pretty good right?

1/21/2022

Ok so I'm trying to analyze my feelings. I'm trying to figure it out. It might be complicated, but maybe it is simple. I'm still trying to figure it out. I think it is simple, I mean, feelings are pretty simple. I'm trying to figure out how feelings work or function in the mind.

1/28/2022

Ok so I'm trying to figure this out. Academics can be pretty complicated, however it seems like I know everything I need to know. I mean I know about the mental processes. They are emotion, thinking, problem solving, memory, learning, language, knowledge, mental representations, concepts, mental categories, decision making, deciding, reasoning, choice, automaticity, insight, self-knowledge, creativity, attention, awareness. Those mental processes are really important, it's also important to understand them. I understand how the mind works because I understand those mental processes.

So what else do I need to understand? I understand that some feelings can be more powerful or intellectual, that is when they might be like emotions, because one definition of emotion is 'any strong feeling'. I don't know if a primary emotion comes first and occurs for a few seconds before a secondary emotion follows. I mean, feelings can be pretty complicated, is the feeling complicated first and then becomes simple later? It has been said that feelings are the result of emotions, so that means that first emotions occur and then a simple or secondary feeling follows after.

Um so if i understand that stuff about feelings and thoughts and mental processes then what else would I need to understand in order to function. I've looked at some logic textbooks so I can think clearly.

1/31/2022

Ok so i'm trying to figure out how I got to this point. I mean, I can think clearly and stuff right, the only question is how did I get here? What did I need to analyze? I figured out that cognitive science would call that an idea that the person is thinking about, an idea or a concept that the person is thinking about.

So people think with a stream of thought that involves thinking about different or various concepts. In order to think clearly the person would have to have a good understanding of clear concepts, or what clear concepts are like. That way the stream of thoughts that they have could have clear concepts, and the person would know that.

So um, they know what a concept is. They know how to think about information and think clearly, what else would they need to know?

4/4/2022

So what else do I need to figure out. I think I have a pretty good understanding of everything. I did a lot of research and taught people a lot of stuff. They were educated so by me teaching them I got their response as an academic. That taught me their perspective of the information I was figuring out.

4/6/2020

So there is a relationship between emotion and cognition. Cognition is thought or thinking while emotion just involves feelings. So people can either feel things or think about things. Thoughts can be about things or thoughts can direct actions. A thought that directs an action is just doing physical stuff that you can control, or is under your control. That is the difference between voluntary and involuntary movements, voluntary movements are under your control so you must use thoughts or thinking to control them.

That makes me wonder, what is the difference between thoughts and thinking? Thinking could use words and sentences while other thoughts could be non-verbal. A thought does not have to use words. People can think things and not use words, though words could help other thoughts.

That is how people control their actions, they use thoughts to control their actions or behavior, sometimes the thoughts are sentences while other times they do not use words at all.

So I did a lot of research. What did I learn again. I'm really smart now, I understand cognitive science. It was more complicated than I initially thought. I can try to briefly describe it. There is cognitive load, which is the processing your mind does. Vision creates a cognitive load on your mind. That's like asking how many megabytes does vision cause your mind to process. Vision uses a cognitive load on your mind. The other senses are also processed by your mind. Is that all there is to how the mind works? I can just describe how the mind works by comparing it to how a computer works, the mind is like a computer that way.

An Assessment of the Nature of Feeling and Thought
By
Mark Pettinelli

When we have a feeling in the mind, what is the nature of that feeling? Does it start at some point, and end at another point? Are we aware when the feeling starts and stops also? I guess the feeling could start at any second and end at any other second. What else is there to notice about that feeling?

The feeling could also be conscious or unconscious. A conscious feeling would be more clear to you, while an unconscious feeling you might not notice as easily. The question is, how much does the person care about that feeling? Caring about a feeling is important, the person could make an appraisal, or an assessment of their emotions.

An appraisal is when a person makes an assessment of their emotional state. Or they make an assessment of what their emotions are and what caused those emotions. The appraisal is done with thoughts and is cognitive, while it's about their emotions.

That is what an appraisal of emotion is, when someone makes an assessment of what caused their emotions and what the resulting emotions are. For instance I might guess what I am feeling and what caused those feelings. That's all an appraisal is, it's an assessment of your emotions and what might have caused them.

When humans have an emotion, what is the nature of that emotion? Also, is the person aware that the emotion is occurring? I said that they could make an assessment of what they are feeling, if they are having an emotion or feeling, and when that feeling starts and stops.

There is also a difference between emotions and feelings. For instance a feeling could be more direct and tangible, while an emotion could be stronger but might be more distant, or you might not be as in touch with the emotion as you are with the feeling. However, if the emotion is stronger, wouldn't you be more in touch with it?

I mean, is feeling just about how strong the feeling is, and emotions are just stronger feelings? Or can a feeling be more clear to you at one point, and less clear at another? Maybe feelings are more clear feelings that you are more aware of, and emotions are deeper. Feelings could be very strong then, and emotions could be more distant.

I mean, the question is, how do feelings feel in the mind? I said that a feeling could be clear to the person, and an emotion could be less clear or dulled down, but stronger. Also, emotions could be more like thoughts, or more intellectual, while feelings could be more like sensations, and more direct. That is why they are called feelings after all, because you can "feel" them.

So the question is, once again, how do feelings feel in the mind? Does a feeling start at one point, and end at another second or point? And is the person aware that this is happening?

I mean is a feeling conscious to the person or is the feeling more unconscious?

That is basically how the mind works, either there are feelings or thoughts, what else could be going on in the mind that a person should be aware of anyway? I mean either they are having a feeling or a thought.

So once again, what then is the difference between feelings and emotions. Or I guess the point is to figure out what feelings feel like in the mind. Is a feeling something that you are in touch with, or is a feeling something that you are less in touch with and it could be more unconscious. I guess the point is how does that feeling feel. It could start at one second and end at another second, that's a pretty clear description of how a feeling feels. But is feeling that simple? I mean is a feeling just something that you feel that starts at one second and ends at another second? Or is a feeling more complicated than that. I mean, could a person be having multiple feelings that they could be more or less conscious of or aware of?

I mean, what am I feeling right now, how complicated is that? How complicated are my feelings right now, that is an interesting question. Are my feelings clear, or are they more unconscious, or are they intellectual, or are they stupid?

I guess when I describe it that way feelings can be pretty simple, I mean, it's mostly just that a feeling starts at one second and ends at some other point in time. There could also be multiple feelings occurring at once, that seems pretty simple.

So what else do I need to add about how feelings feel. I mean, how am I supposed to describe how I am feeling right now. I feel happy I guess, but what else is there to that feeling. I mean, when I feel bad is it just a bad feeling, or what else is going on.

Feelings are pretty simple then, I mean there isn't really very much going on with feelings, they just start at one time and then end at some point later on, however long that feeling lasts I suppose.

I mean, in the mind there are feelings and thoughts, both of which are experiences.

I mean, I have feelings and thoughts, that is kind of an obvious statement, everyone has feelings and thoughts.

The question is, am I aware that those feelings are occurring? I mean, I could not notice all of the feelings I am having, if i'm experiencing multiple feelings anyway.

Does it matter if I do an appraisal and make an assessment of my feelings? If I care about the feeling then it might influence how aware I am about the feeling. It might also change the strength of the feeling.

How is that possible? Why would thinking about a feeling change the strength of the feeling? It seems to make sense, I mean thinking about your own feelings creates the feelings by itself. Cognition or thinking is extremely powerful.

How then does that work, when you have a feeling, the feeling could be caused by something real or some external source, or you could make the feeling yourself and it could be something under your control.

How could thinking about a feeling change the feeling? How would that work exactly. I mean, obviously thought is important, when you think about something, then that could be what you are feeling. What would be an example of that. Physical feelings don't seem like they would be under your control, however. Is life mostly just physical feelings then? There are non-physical feelings too, however. What are examples of physical feelings and non-physical feelings then. If I feel scared that could be an intellectual feeling. Other feelings could be happy, excited, depressed or sad. Those feelings don't seem like they could be influenced by just thinking. I mean, people are mostly not in control of what they are feeling. Doing actions and experiencing things could cause feelings that the person is not in control of, however they could think about those feelings. I already said that they can make appraisals of feelings, which are assessments of the nature of the feelings and what might have caused those feelings.

So what is an example of a happy feeling, there is also stimulation, or how much power your mind has. Stimulation is interesting, for instance I sometimes am bored and that causes anxiety or pain, then I usually need to do something to occupy myself. So stimulation is different from feelings, for instance the mind could be fine with just stimulation and not even experiencing any feelings at all. Or is feeling a combination of feeling and stimulation, I mean the stimulation feels like something. Could stimulation feel happy then, since it could be making the person less bored? That makes a lot of sense, I should try to get more stimulation then so I can feel more happy. There is also thought power, that is kind of like asking how many megabytes your visual of the world is, the steady visual that seeing brings must have a cognitive load on your mind that provides stimulation just from vision, there's also the other senses that provide input and stimulation.

So what then is the difference between feelings and emotions?

Feelings are more conscious right, I mean both feelings and emotions are felt, and they feel like something, but what then is the difference between them? I guess the question is how do feelings feel in the mind. I said that feelings could be either conscious or unconscious, or stupid or intellectual. Are feelings more like sensations that are more direct and conscious and some of them could be more stupid than an emotion.

So is emotion just strong feelings? Or is emotion more intellectual than feelings. I'm trying to describe the difference between feelings and emotions. Or i'm just trying to describe how feelings feel in the mind. Feelings can feel stupid if they are like physical sensations right. Emotions could be more powerful then but they might be more powerful in an intellectual way

Um so i'm getting a little bit confused here, i'm trying to describe how feelings feel in the mind right. I mean, how complicated is that? A feeling can feel stupid or intellectual, or a feeling could be something that is direct or indirect. If the feeling is stupid it might be more direct like the sensations. If a feeling is indirect then it could be intellectual. Um so what does that mean for how feelings feel in the mind then. This is getting a little bit complicated. A feeling could be more or less conscious, or it could be stupid or intellectual. So it could be conscious and stupid, or conscious and intellectual, or it could be unconscious and stupid or intellectual. That is kind of interesting. So once again, how do feelings feel in the mind? I'm trying to describe all of the ways a feeling can be experienced. Like what if I tried to describe how I am feeling right now, how could I do that. I feel happy I guess and I also have physical sensations. I am in my bedroom and I can experience the 5 different sensations of taste, touch, sight, sound and smell. I'm always experiencing those sensations and I'm always thinking about things. I don't really feel very much I guess. Maybe I just don't have a lot of emotions compared to other people. Emotions are strong, while feelings can be weak or strong. If emotions are unconscious, however, then how could they be strong? If I feel happiness then is it unconscious and strong? It is strong if I can feel it, then it would be a strong feeling and not an emotion. When the happiness emotion becomes conscious it becomes a strong feeling. Emotion is either conscious or unconscious, while feelings are always conscious because you can feel them.

So what am I feeling now. I feel happy, that is both an emotion and a feeling because it is unconscious as an emotion, and conscious as a feeling. Or I could say that it is a conscious feeling and an unconscious emotion. When I think about the happiness it becomes more conscious and more of something I can really feel.

So what am I feeling right now, I can start with that analysis. I mean I'm trying to describe the way feelings feel in the mind. I feel happy I guess. I don't really have very many feelings I think. I also have physical sensations that make me happy. I can feel the bed that I am in for instance. There is also my breathing that I can feel. I was taught to focus on my breathing as a coping mechanism for my anxiety. I also learned that by myself by practicing the suggestion to focus on my breath or do deep breathing exercises. So I don't have very many emotions or feelings then. I mean sometimes I get happy when I interact with people, that's kind of important. Those are feelings. When is a feeling unconscious then? I

Would say that feelings are either conscious or unconscious. The goal is to have strong, conscious feelings I would think. I said that an emotion could be unconscious or conscious, while feelings are always conscious. Emotions and feelings can also feel either stupid or intellectual. The physical feelings or sensations are usually more stupid than intellectual feelings or emotions.

Um so how am I supposed to describe how I am feeling right now then? I don't think that feelings are very complicated if you think about them that way. I mean, I don't really have very many feelings to begin with. Maybe other people have more complicated or stronger feelings than I do, I don't really know.

I think i've simplified how feelings feel then. I mean, I am a pretty simple person, my feelings aren't very complicated. My thoughts aren't very complicated with er I would say. I mean, when I have a feeling it is either conscious or unconscious, strong or weak, or stupid or intellectual.

That is a pretty simple explanation of how feelings feel in the mind. I think I've simplified it. But that is a good way to start analyzing your feelings I would think. I start with a simple mind that is clear and not feeling very much, then slowly build up my analysis and awareness of my feelings (also the descriptions of them).

Mental Notes 2 of Mark Pettinelli

File:The selected writings of Mark Pettinelli.pdf - Wikimedia Commons

What is there to know about cognitive psychology? I've memorized the mental processes. They are emotion, thought, problem

solving, decision making, judgment, reasoning, choice, memory, learning, language, mental representations, knowledge, concepts, categories, attention and awareness, creativity, perception, automaticity, insight and self-knowledge.

So what else do I need to know or learn? I mean I think I know everything that I need to understand. There could be more things that I might need to learn, however. I don't really know, I feel like I understand everything that I need to understand.

I don't know if I need to know anything else, I mean I sort of already understand everything I need to know about how the mind works. I know what all the mental processes are, there's about 20 of them that I already listed.

That makes me wonder, what is the difference between thoughts and thinking? Thinking could use words and sentences while other thoughts could be non-verbal. A thought does not have to use words. People can think things and not use words, though words could help other thoughts.

That is how people control their actions, they use thoughts to control their actions or behavior, sometimes the thoughts are sentences while other times they do not use words at all.

So I did a lot of research. What did I learn again? I'm really smart now, I understand cognitive science. It was more complicated than I initially thought. I can try to briefly describe it. There is cognitive load, which is the processing your mind does. Vision creates a cognitive load on your mind. That's like asking how many megabytes does vision cause your mind to process. Vision uses a cognitive load on your mind. The other senses are also processed by your mind. Is that all there is to how the mind works? I can just describe how the mind works by comparing it to how a computer works, the mind is like a computer that way.

Um so I don't know what else I would have to understand. I already understand a lot of stuff. I know what the mental processes are and basic stuff about academics and life. I mean I have a high school education. I understand math and algebra. I know basic things about chemistry and physics. I also can speak a little bit of Spanish as a foreign language. I learned all of that stuff in high school.

After high school I started to study psychology and cognitive science. I spent a lot of time thinking about how the mind works.

Um so what else do I know? I have the high school education I told you about. I learned stuff after high school because I was meeting with therapists who know stuff about psychology, feelings and even cognitive science.

That made me study how the mind works, my therapists knew stuff about that.

Um so what is everything that I know? That's a good question. I already mentioned what I learned in high school. Then I learned stuff about cognitive science and how the mind works after high school. Also other stuff about psychology, or I guess cognitive science is in the same category as psychology.

So what did I learn about psychology? I already pointed out about the mental processes the mind has. There is also other stuff like logic and clear thinking. There's also the interaction between emotion and cognition. Thinking and feeling interact in the mind. How does that happen exactly?

Thoughts can influence feelings, and feelings can influence thoughts also. That is pretty simple actually. It's important to know, however. FOr instance people can control or influence their feelings and emotions with their thinking and thoughts. Cognition is the person's thinking and feelings and emotions are what the person is feeling.

Maybe there's stuff about logical thinking and reasoning that I can learn. There's also stuff about feelings and consciousness that I can learn from those 5 different books by Damasio. I also have a couple books on the world's greatest speeches.

So what about logic and clear thinking would I need to learn? There doesn't seem to be very much involved with clear thinking, I mean it seems kind of obvious how to think clearly, I don't know if I need to point out anything.

Maybe I need to point out stuff about clear thinking, on the other hand, I've always been a clear thinker even as a child. Having more emotions now shouldn't interfere with my thinking, I mean I can still think clearly even though I have strong emotions.

I mean, I've been clear thinking all the many years of my life, it's not like thinking is new to me, I've been doing it for a long time now lol.

I mean, I'm not stupid, I know how to think clearly without any errors or misunderstandings.

I think logically and intelligently, I don't need to understand anything else.

So what pieces of knowledge would I also need to know or understand. I already pointed out that I understand the mental processes.

Ok so I'm trying to do an account of what's happened and what I want to achieve with my life. I'm bored most of the time, but I don't know if there is a solution to that. I mean interacting with people is kind of difficult, maybe I can work on that so I could interact with other people more as an activity. That seems like a good idea.

I don't know how I'm going to do that exactly. I can think clearly and know how my mind works, so I can function, but interacting with other humans might be difficult.

It's good that I can function so that means I can function when I'm interacting with other people, you know, put my skills to use in a practical fashion.

Um so, I'm trying to keep track of everything I know and everything I might need to know or learn in the future. What do I know now? I understand how the mind works, I think. I don't know what else I might need to know. I mean I understand that there is feeling and thought, two separate mental processes. When someone thinks about something, how is feeling involved?

I mean, feeling can be involved with thinking, feelings can assist thoughts I would think. How exactly does that happen. I think feelings can help to motivate thoughts. There is feeling and thinking, what is the difference between those two mental processes? Feelings you can feel, and people can also feel thoughts, however thoughts are sentences or words, while feelings are just feelings. What is the difference between a thought that uses words and a thought that does not use words then? Words are really important then, words help people think about whatever it is that they want to think about.

So say I want to think about something, are words always involved? Feelings are different from thoughts then. Feelings are when you feel something, and thoughts are when you think about something. What is the difference between feeling and thought then? I mean I can think about a person, or I could have feelings about that person.

Feelings are different from thoughts then. Feelings feel like something, while thoughts are more informative. If i have a thought, it is an idea or a piece of information or a concept, while feelings are things you can feel.

So thought is basically thinking, while feeling is experiencing feelings. What is the difference between the two then? What is thinking? Thinking uses words or ideas and concepts, while feeling is just emotional.

So thinking is just thoughts, while feelings are emotions. THinking just involves thinking about stuff, while feeling involves feeling things that are emotional, versus thinking about something that is intellectual like an idea or a concept or a sentence.

THinking is thinking about stuff, while feeling is feeling stuff. Um so I don't know if that's a very good description. Thinking about things involves thought, while feeling just involves experiencing feelings. Thoughts can be words or sentences, or ideas or concepts. Does thought always have to be a sentence? It seems like it's more conscious if it's a sentence or thought about with words. Words are sounds in the head that mean something or have a definition.

It seems like thoughts need to be thought about with words in order for them to be conscious. I don't have to always think with words, however. I can think fine without thinking sentences to myself.

Feelings can play a role in decision making, or they could play a role in the construction of the self, or in the person being conscious and aware. There is also how feelings feel by themselves, or the study of the nature of feelings.

So what else do I need to explore here, there's feelings and thoughts. I mean I know when I'm thinking or when i'm experiencing feelings. That is kind of important to know.

I like having feelings and thoughts, it gives me an experience of something. There is also the senses. Is that all that humans feel? They can feel thoughts, feelings, and sensory inputs.

So what then is the difference between sensory inputs and feelings and thoughts? Feelings and thoughts are internal cognitive processes while sensory inputs are sensory inputs. They come from outside the mind, taste, touch, sight, sound and smell are all inputs from the external environment, while feelings and thoughts and internal mental processes.

I want to do more research, what else could I try to figure out?

So I don't know what else I might need to learn, this article covers most of the material I need to know. I explained the difference between emotions and feelings in my "the selected writings of Mark Pettinelli" book. The difference is that emotions are main and primary, they occur first possibly for just a few seconds, then there is a conscious feeling as a secondary feeling.

THe main emotions are happy, sad, anger, fear, surprise and disgust. THose emotions occur first and then there is a secondary feeling. I don't know how long those main emotions last, possibly for just a few seconds though I would think they could last longer and be mixed in with the secondary feelings that are a result of those primary emotions. I mean feelings and emotions can be used interchangeably, it's kind of complicated to describe what someone is feeling.

So what else do I need to describe, feelings and thoughts are mental phenomena, they occur inside the brain. The brain as a whole contributes other mental processes that contribute to consciousness. I already listed the mental processes at the beginning of this article.

Those mental processes combined contribute to and form a humans consciousness. Those mental processes are also present in other animals and forms of life, for the most part.

Final Notes by Mark Pettinelli

So what else do I need to figure out? These are my final notes that I won't include in my book. I don't know what else I might need to learn.

Um, so I think I know everything I need to know in order to function. I don't think I need to know anything else. I can think clearly and logically and can function.

So I'm really excited, other people are conscious.

I'm still going through some books. I'll add the information that I learn here. I don't know if there's anything else I need to learn.

I mean, what else would I need to know? I can function fine, I don't even know if I already said that. Now I'm being guided, but I wrote that final book by myself. These are notes about other stuff I would want to learn. That makes sense, they didn't have the academics figured out until I finished explaining some academics. I was providing a critical contribution to the academics that they needed for a long time and to finally finish the academics.

I don't know what the other people who were contributing to the academics had to offer, but I was part of the small number of people who were contributing to the academics and working together with other academics to figure everything out. I don't know what they're trying to research now, my part in that is over.

One of my final ideas was that thought is different from feeling. **Feelings and thoughts can also influence each other. Now I keep track of my feelings and my thoughts so I can be intelligent, conscious and logical.**

I've always been logical and clear thinking but I wasn't that smart before I did all this research over the last decade.

So I'm just going to post here what else I might need or can learn that I think might be valuable information, but I'm being guided so it won't be posted as part of my last book "THe selected writings of Mark Pettinelli".

SO I don't know what else I might need to know, I'm still reading books and thinking about stuff. **My last insight was that people think and feel at the same time, and they can keep track of those feelings and thoughts.**

It's important to note that people can think and feel at the same time. They can also keep track of those feelings and thoughts, and if feelings lead to thoughts and if thoughts lead to feelings.

Um so what else would I need to know? It's kind of important to keep track of your feelings and thoughts.

I don't know if there's anything else I need to learn then. Maybe I'm just done with the research. I mean, if I can keep track of my feelings and thoughts and can function in a practical manner, and think clearly and logically, then I don't know what else I would need to achieve.

I'm functioning perfectly fine right now. I keep track of my feelings and thoughts and how I'm doing in general. I can think clearly and logically, so all that works.

Um, so I need to think more about that. I wrote a lot about the difference between feelings and emotions. I concluded that the mix of feelings that people feel can be complicated, and that there is no set definition between the difference of feelings and emotions, that it is kind of subjective and can be defined in various ways, the important part just being how the person feels, whatever their feelings or emotions or thoughts are doing at that time.

Um so that seems like a pretty good explanation. I don't know what else I would need to figure out or analyze.

Consciousness is important. There might be information about consciousness that I might need to learn or research.

I don't know what else I might need to know. I understand how the mind thinks about stuff, that seems like a good understanding.

I also understand how the mind feels, the mind feels emotions and feelings all the time.

Um so i don't know what else i might need to figure out. It seems like I know everything that I need to understand. I mean I know about the mental processes and **I know about thinking and feeling. There is also perception, memory, language, judgment and reasoning and choice, learning, attention and awareness, categories, knowledge, mental representations and concepts, problem solving and decision making.and creativity, automaticity, insight and self knowledge.**

Um so what else would I need to understand about consciousness or feelings and how they function in the mind? I mean I understand how feelings work and I understand how consciousness works. Consciousness is all the mental processes working together to form a picture of how the mind functions. THen the person becomes conscious of their feelings and thoughts and other mental functions.

So feelings and thoughts contribute to the persons consciousness. I mean, what is it to say that the person is conscious anyway? I mean I guess it's just awareness right. Attention and awareness are 2 of the mind's mental processes.

So what exactly is consciousness? Being conscious and aware I guess. Conscious means aware I would think, so if someone is conscious it means that they are aware of themselves or their environment or their mind.

Um so what else do i need to understand in order to function? I mean I can feel my emotions and my feelings and know when I am thinking. Is there anything else I would need to know? I mean, what else is there behind understanding consciousness? I guess I would have to keep track of all of my feelings and thoughts to be aware in general.

If I do that then I think I should be pretty good and well off. I mean i think I just need to do that, keep track of my feelings and thoughts and behaviors. Seems pretty simple. I mean, I don't know the biology of it but still understand how it works.

Consciousness can be pretty complicated, for instance what is consciousness, what does it feels like to feel something? I mean I guess consciousness is just the sum total of our mental processes. So consciousness is just the combination of our attention and awareness, sometimes our memory and sometimes we use our language. It is also the combination of our thoughts and our feelings, whatever it is we are feeling at the moment and if we are thinking about something. I mean, thought and feeling are probably the two greatest contributions to consciousness. What else could be going on other than thinking about something and feeling something? We could also be more or less aware and attentive. We could be using our judgment or making decisions or problem solving. What are some of the other mental processes that our consciousness could be using? We could be learning something, We could be trying to figure something out or problem solve.

So consciousness is just basically what we are aware of, or if we are aware in general. A lot of things contribute to our awareness or our consciousness, like whatever we are aware of at any moment. Humans are aware of their thoughts and feelings and other mental functions like memory and attention and awareness, language and knowledge and concepts, their thinking processes and feeling processes, so whatever they are feeling they could be aware of.

What else is there to understanding consciousness? Someone could have a thought, that would make them aware of whatever the thought is about right. Feelings can also be about stuff, for instance if you feel happy there might be a reason you feel that way. What else is complicated about feelings and thoughts, i previously said that feelings and thoughts make a person more conscious right. Feelings and thoughts can be caused by something or be connected to something, like a behavior or another feeling or thought. That's important for consciousness if you think about it because our feelings and thoughts help make us more aware. But what then is consciousness? Consciousness is our awareness of our feelings and thoughts and other mental processes. If a person is aware of their feelings and thoughts then they are conscious right. If someone is having feelings and thoughts then the person could be a conscious person, but they wouldn't be as conscious as someone who is aware of their feelings and thoughts.

I mean, so what is consciousness then? How aware a person is of their environment or their mind. In order for someone to be aware of their mind or environment they would have to be aware of their mental processes like feelings and thoughts. Those are probably the two most significant mental processes. So how aware someone is of their feelings and thoughts makes the person more conscious and aware. It makes them aware of what they are feeling and thinking, and their other mental processes like language, memory, attention and awareness. So someone could be aware of how aware they are, or if they are using language or speaking, or using their memory. If a person is aware of any of that stuff then they would be more aware of what their mind is doing. A person could also be aware of what is going on in their environment.

A person could be aware of what they are thinking about also, the more aware they are of what they are thinking about the more conscious they would be because they would be aware of their own mind and their environment.

I need to simplify that. Consciousness is a persons awareness of their mind or their environment. So if someone is aware of what their mind is doing then they would be more conscious. They could also be aware of their environment, the environment could be influencing or causing the person's mind to feel or think things. So what is consciousness then? A person could be conscious of their mind and what it is doing. It could be experiencing any of the mental processes such as attention, awareness, memory, learning, language, feeling, thinking, problem solving, decision making, perception, insight, creativity, knowledge, concepts, mental representations, the use of categories, or other mental processes. all of those mental processes are things the mind does. So consciousness would be if someone is aware of what their mind is doing. One thing a mind could be doing is experiencing the mental processes I just listed.

A person could be aware of what they are feeling or thinking or whatever it is they are experiencing. That makes them more conscious because it is what they are experiencing or feeling. Most of the mental processes contribute to the persons feelings or thoughts. A person could be aware of what they are feeling. just feeling something is different from being aware of those feelings. It could be that someone has a feeling that thcy are not aware of. I guess that could involve various degrees of awareness.

that seems complicated, for instance what does it mean to be aware of a feeling or thought or aware of something in the real world? That is actually pretty simple, it is just how aware someone is of what they are feeling or thinking, or whatever else their mind might be doing. The mind can also experience things from their environment, but those things get experienced in the mind.

That seems like a more simple explanation of consciousness. Consciousness is just the awareness of a person's feelings and thoughts and other things the mind can do or experience.

That seems like a pretty good explanation of consciousness. Either someone is feeling something or thinking about something, and they can be aware of what they are thinking or feeling. Whatever the person's mind is doing they could be aware of. For instance they could be aware of a feeling that they are having. They could be aware of thoughts that they are having. If they are trying to figure something out then they know they are doing that. They could also know about the feelings that they are having at any moment. I can feel things right now and I'm aware of those feelings. I'm aware that I have feelings and thoughts. I am perfectly aware of my feelings and how I feel all the time or just in general.

So what else do I need to learn?

I mean, what about those 2 topics of intelligence and emotion would I need to learn about? I already understand things about consciousness and emotion and cognition. I mean, in order to function I don't really need to understand anything, for instance when I was in high school and the previous years of school I didn't know anything but had feelings and thoughts.

What have I learned about feelings and thoughts anyway? I have those 2 articles that I wrote where I talk about the difference between feelings and emotions. I said that feelings can be more simple and direct and possibly more stupid than emotions, and that emotions could be more powerful but more intellectual and complex. For instance sensory figure out? That is an excellent question. There's stuff about intelligence I can learn, and stuff about emotion that I can learn. What kind of information about intellect could I learn, and what kind of information about emotions or feelings might I nlings are not emotions they are feelings.

So what else might I need to know about feelings and thoughts?

I mean, some feelings are intellectual while other feelings are more stupid. Like sensory feelings are stupid while some thoughts could be more intelligent. Some feelings might even be intelligent feelings, it's kind of hard to describe how someone is feeling at any moment if you think about it.

I mean, what have I learned about feelings and thoughts anyway? There isn't really that much I need to know about them. I mean, I can describe how I am feeling at any given time. I also know how to think about things. What else would I need to do in order to function? That seems like it's enough. I mean, what else do I need to know about feelings and thoughts? In high school I had feelings and thoughts and was functioning perfectly fine, I don't know what else I might need to know or learn. I can function, and I have feelings and thoughts. I can describe how I feel at any moment. I mean, what else is there to functioning? Clear thinking is actually pretty simple.

I mean, how does intellect or intelligence work exactly? And how does emotion function? What causes feelings to start or stop and how does the mind think about thoughts? Is there just a thought process or something, or a feeling process that goes along with the thought process?

Um so what else would I need to know about how emotions or thoughts function in the mind? It seems like how feelings work is a simple process, and how thoughts work is also a simple process

I mean, either someone is thinking something, or feeling something, or both at the same time. Seems fairly simple, I mean, what is involved with a thought process anyway, it seems like it's just a stream of thought, and an emotion process is just a stream of feelings. That seems like all that is going on in any emotional activity.

So what else would I need to study anyway? There is consciousness and emotion, there is also thought or cognition. What else is important that the mind does? It doesn't look like the mind does much else. Emotion and cognition and the resulting consciousness are the main things that the mind does. I don't know what else could be considered important.

THere's the autonomic nervous system, which is basically the functions the body does automatically or involuntarily.

THere's the effect of interruptions, and the limited capacity of the cognitive system or the mind.

There's appraisal theory or the way the mind cognitively interprets events.

Cognitive-autonomic theory

I mean, what role do cognitive evaluations play in how emotion and thought is experienced? People think about what happened around them and how it makes them feel all the time, so the question is how do these evaluations influence their emotions?

It seems pretty simple if you think about it, i mean basically nothing complicated is happening, there's the stimulus, then the resulting emotions or cognitive evaluations.

And there is the physical body that produces sensations and reactions that can influence emotions and feelings. So is a feeling physical or is it mental and psychological?

I mean, there's the effect of cognitive evaluations. So what else is there, I mean, people experience a steady state of feeling. Their feelings could be interrupted by thoughts that they could have. That seems pretty simple if you think about it.

So how does the emotion process work exactly? There is a stimulus, something that causes the person to have an emotion, then the person might think about the stimulus and what feelings it might have caused, so do the feelings come before the person makes an assessment or after the assessment? I suppose a person could have feelings at the same time they are making an assessment, and what they think or what their assessment is can change how they are feeling.

So the feelings and the assessment both occur right after some stimulus that caused them to have those feelings and thoughts. The assessment or what they think about the stimulus can change the feelings they are having at the same time they are having feelings from the stimulus.

So there's a stimulus, something that causes feelings, then the feelings follow and those feelings can be influenced by thoughts that the person can have, which can generate new feelings or change the feelings caused by the input (the stimulus).

These are my mental notes. I'm going to discuss my mental notes in this document.

So what else do I need to figure out? That is an excellent question lol.

I already know the 21 mental processes, they are emotion, thought, judgment, reasoning, choice, memory, learning, language, perception, creativity, problem solving, decision making, categories, mental representations, knowledge, concepts, awareness, attention, automaticity, insight and self-knowledge (which is the beliefs people have about themselves).

So I know all of those processes, it's kind of important to know those because they form a picture of how the mind functions.

Um so what else would I need to know or understand?

What is my current understanding anyway, like what do I already know?
I know a lot of stuff actually, i mean i know how to function, think and feel, those are kind of important things to know. Feelings are different from thoughts anyway. Feelings are experiences of feeling or emotion, while thoughts are ideas or concepts that someone can think about.
Then there's just basic functioning but that just involves using your thoughts and feelings in a practical manner, which I can do without a problem.
Um so if i can function then what else would i need to understand, that's an excellent question.

I mean, what is behind my actions? As a child I did not have a lot of knowledge of the world but was functioning perfectly fine. I'm still mostly the same i would say except i understand feelings and thoughts and consciousness.

For instance, as a child I did not understand what the word 'emotion regulation' meant. When I came across it I was confused.

Now I understand that it's about managing and maintaining your own emotions, as a child I did not influence my emotions very much. I mean, I had feelings but it was a fairly simple process.

Um, so that seems like a pretty good run down or explanation of how the mind works. I don't know what else I would need to explain. There's feelings and thoughts, and emotion regulation. There is practical functioning and different kinds of feelings.

So what else do I need to know? I know that I have feelings and thoughts, that's pretty much all i need to know i think, what else would i need to know or understand?
So that's really interesting. I can experience feelings all the time and think about stuff all of the time.

Thoughts can be verbal or non-verbal. Thoughts can direct actions or be used to think about things.

I don't know what else I might need to know then. I think clearly and feel stuff, what else is there to living and being conscious anyway?

Ok so i can just go back to my baseline, what are those feelings and thoughts like anyway, i mean, I have a steady stream of feelings and thoughts all of the time, seems pretty simple if you think about it, I mean, what would i need to know or understand in order to function and think and feel anyway?

So what else would I have to say about emotions, or how emotions function in the mind? It seems like a pretty simple process anyway, I don't know what else I would need to explain about it anyway. I mean, emotions are pretty simple if you think about it.

Thoughts are also simple if you think about it. What about thought is simple anyway?

So what else do I need to know or figure out or understand anyway? I mean, I have a good understanding of how emotions and thoughts work, that's a good explanation of how the mind works in general. I mean, mostly it's just thoughts and feelings, though there is also attention, memory, language, learning, judgment, reasoning, choice, deciding, problem solving, mental representations, concepts, categories, knowledge, automaticity, insight, self-knowledge, awareness, creativity, perception,

So what else would I need to learn or understand? It seems like I have a good enough understanding of how the mind works and how feelings and emotions function anyway. What else would there be for my analysis or explanation anyway? I mean I understand how the mind works and I understand what the mental processes are anyway.

So what else would I need to understand about emotions and how emotions function anyway? Emotions are pretty simple if you think about it. I don't know what could be complicated about emotions anyway.

So I need to do an overview of the information, like what exactly do I need to learn about how the mind works anyway, I feel like I have a good understanding of how the mind works, for instance there are feelings and thoughts in the mind that runs through a person's consciousness all of the time. That's important to understand, I think. What else could be going on in the mind? There's the other mental processes like attention, learning and language and memory and awareness, judgment, reasoning and choice, problem solving and decision making, there's mental representations, concepts, categories and knowledge, creativity and perception, and automaticity, insight and self knowledge.

Those are all important to understand, I think.

I mean, what am I going to learn if I do more reading anyway? I already know that there are feelings and thoughts in the mind,

There's feeling 'states' and logical 'states'. For instance someone could be thinking clearly and logically about something or in a logical thinking type of state.

Emotions are feelings.

An emotion is a mental mode.

Cognitive, evaluative and motivational

So what else would I need to understand about how emotion works in the mind anyway? Seems pretty simple anyway. I mean, there's different emotional states and different emotions and feelings someone can experience.

So someone could go into different emotional states or something. People can feel a ton of different things and experience lots of different feelings and even thoughts which are more intellectual.

www.ingramcontent.com/pod-product-compliance
Lightning Source LLC
Chambersburg PA
CBHW070151310326
41914CB00089B/780